R Deep Learning Essentials

Build automatic classification and prediction models
using unsupervised learning

Dr. Joshua F. Wiley

[PACKT] open source ✳
P U B L I S H I N G   community experience distilled

BIRMINGHAM - MUMBAI

R Deep Learning Essentials

First published: March 2016

Production reference: 1220316

Published by Packt Publishing Ltd.
Livery Place
35 Livery Street
Birmingham B3 2PB, UK.

ISBN 978-1-78528-058-0

www.packtpub.com

Credits

Author
Dr. Joshua F. Wiley

Reviewer
Vincenzo Lomonaco

Commissioning Editor
Akram Hussain

Acquisition Editor
Manish Nainani

Content Development Editor
Siddhesh Salvi

Technical Editor
Pranil Pathare

Copy Editor
Stephen Copestake

Project Coordinator
Nidhi Joshi

Proofreader
Safis Editing

Indexer
Mariammal Chettiyar

Graphics
Kirk D'Penha

Disha Haria

Jason Monteiro

Production Coordinator
Conidon Miranda

Cover Work
Conidon Miranda

About the Author

Dr. Joshua F. Wiley is a lecturer at Monash University and a senior partner at Elkhart Group Limited, a statistical consultancy. He earned his PhD from the University of California, Los Angeles. His research focuses on using advanced quantitative methods to understand the complex interplays of psychological, social, and physiological processes in relation to psychological and physical health. In statistics and data science, Joshua focuses on biostatistics and is interested in reproducible research and graphical displays of data and statistical models. Through consulting at Elkhart Group Limited and his former work at the UCLA Statistical Consulting Group, Joshua has helped a wide array of clients, ranging from experienced researchers to biotechnology companies. He develops or codevelops a number of R packages including `varian`, a package to conduct Bayesian scale-location structural equation models, and `MplusAutomation`, a popular package that links R to the commercial Mplus software.

> I would like to thank my wife and family for the years of support and encouragement that have kept me passionate about my work.

About the Reviewer

Vincenzo Lomonaco was born in San Giovanni Rotondo (FG), Italy, in 1991. He spent his childhood in Basilicata and, after getting his scientific lyceum diploma, he moved to Modena. After less than three years, he graduated cum laude in computer science. Attracted by the great reputation and research activities in Bologna, he decided to start his masters in computer science there. In 2015, he graduated cum laude with the dissertation, *Deep Learning for Computer Vision: A comparison between Convolutional Neural Networks and Hierarchical Temporal Memories on object recognition tasks*. He's currently a PhD student at University of Bologna, working on deep learning and biologically-inspired pattern recognition.

www.PacktPub.com

eBooks, discount offers, and more

Did you know that Packt offers eBook versions of every book published, with PDF and ePub files available? You can upgrade to the eBook version at www.PacktPub.com and as a print book customer, you are entitled to a discount on the eBook copy. Get in touch with us at customercare@packtpub.com for more details.

At www.PacktPub.com, you can also read a collection of free technical articles, sign up for a range of free newsletters and receive exclusive discounts and offers on Packt books and eBooks.

https://www2.packtpub.com/books/subscription/packtlib

Do you need instant solutions to your IT questions? PacktLib is Packt's online digital book library. Here, you can search, access, and read Packt's entire library of books.

Why subscribe?

- Fully searchable across every book published by Packt
- Copy and paste, print, and bookmark content
- On demand and accessible via a web browser

Table of Contents

Preface   iii

Chapter 1: Getting Started with Deep Learning   1
  What is deep learning?   2
    Conceptual overview of neural networks   2
    Deep neural networks   6
  R packages for deep learning   8
    Setting up reproducible results   9
    Neural networks   12
    The deepnet package   12
    The darch package   13
    The H2O package   13
  Connecting R and H2O   13
    Initializing H2O   14
    Linking datasets to an H2O cluster   15
  Summary   17

Chapter 2: Training a Prediction Model   19
  Neural networks in R   19
    Building a neural network   20
    Generating predictions from a neural network   35
  The problem of overfitting data – the consequences explained   37
  Use case – build and apply a neural network   40
  Summary   45

Chapter 3: Preventing Overfitting   47
  L1 penalty   48
    L1 penalty in action   50
  L2 penalty   52
    L2 penalty in action   53
    Weight decay (L2 penalty in neural networks)   54

Ensembles and model averaging	57
Use case – improving out-of-sample model performance using dropout	60
Summary	65
Chapter 4: Identifying Anomalous Data	**67**
Getting started with unsupervised learning	68
How do auto-encoders work?	69
Regularized auto-encoders	70
Penalized auto-encoders	70
Denoising auto-encoders	71
Training an auto-encoder in R	71
Use case – building and applying an auto-encoder model	84
Fine-tuning auto-encoder models	88
Summary	93
Chapter 5: Training Deep Prediction Models	**95**
Getting started with deep feedforward neural networks	96
Common activation functions – rectifiers, hyperbolic tangent, and maxout	98
Picking hyperparameters	100
Training and predicting new data from a deep neural network	104
Use case – training a deep neural network for automatic classification	112
Working with model results	123
Summary	130
Chapter 6: Tuning and Optimizing Models	**131**
Dealing with missing data	132
Solutions for models with low accuracy	135
Grid search	135
Random search	137
Summary	149
Appendix: Bibliography	**151**
Index	**153**

Preface

This book is about how to train and use deep learning models or deep neural networks in the R programming language and environment. This book is not intended to provide an in-depth theoretical coverage of deep neural networks, but it will give you enough background to help you understand their basics and use and interpret the results. This book will also show you some of the packages and functions available to train deep neural networks, optimize their hyperparameters to improve the accuracy of your model, and generate predictions or otherwise *use the model you built.* The book is intended to provide an easy-to-read coverage of the essentials in order to get going with real-life examples and applications.

What this book covers

Chapter 1, Getting Started with Deep Learning, shows how to get the R and H2O packages set up and installed on a computer or server along with covering all the basic concepts related to deep learning.

Chapter 2, Training a Prediction Model, covers how to build a shallow unsupervised neural network prediction model.

Chapter 3, Preventing Overfitting, explains different approaches that can be used to prevent models from overfitting the data in order to improve generalizability called regularization on unsupervised data.

Chapter 4, Identifying Anomalous Data, covers how to perform unsupervised deep learning in order to identify anomalous data, such as fraudulent activity or outliers.

Chapter 5, Training Deep Prediction Models, shows how to train deep neural networks to solve prediction and classification problems, such as image recognition.

Chapter 6, Tuning and Optimizing Models, explains how to adjust model tuning parameters to improve and optimize the accuracy and performance of deep learning models.

Appendix, Bibliography, contains the references for all the citations throughout the book.

What you need for this book

You do not need much to use for this book. The main piece of software that you need is R, which is open source and runs on Windows, Mac OS, and many varieties of Linux. You will also need a recent version of Java. Once you have R and Java installed, you will need to install some R packages, all of which work on every major operating system.

Perhaps, the more challenging requirement is that, for any real deep learning application, and even to explore quite small examples, modern hardware is required. For this book, I primarily used a desktop with an Intel Xeon E5-2670 v2 running at 2.50 GHz (10 physical cores, 20 logical cores), with 32 GB of memory, and a Samsung 850 PRO 512GB SSD. You do not necessarily need an equivalent system, but I found that running some examples on a latest laptop with 16 GB of memory and a dual core i7 processor is time consuming.

Who this book is for

This book caters to aspiring data scientists who are well-versed with machine learning concepts with R and are looking to explore the deep learning paradigm using the packages available in R. You should have a fundamental understanding of the R language and be comfortable with statistical algorithms and machine learning techniques, but you do not need to be well-versed with deep learning concepts.

Conventions

In this book, you will find a number of text styles that distinguish between different kinds of information. Here are some examples of these styles and an explanation of their meaning.

Code words in text, database table names, folder names, filenames, file extensions, pathnames, dummy URLs, user input, and Twitter handles are shown as follows: "Of course, we cannot actually use the `library()` function until we have installed the packages."

A block of code is set as follows:

```
## uncomment to install the checkpoint package
## install.packages("checkpoint")
library(checkpoint)

checkpoint("2016-02-20", R.version = "3.2.3")
```

When we wish to draw your attention to a particular part of a code block, the relevant lines or items are set in bold:

```
performance.outsample[,-4]
```

	Size	Maxit	Shuffle	Accuracy	AccuracyLower	AccuracyUpper
1	40	60	**FALSE**	**0.93**	**0.92**	**0.94**
2	20	100	FALSE	0.92	0.91	0.93
3	20	100	TRUE	0.92	0.91	0.93
4	50	100	FALSE	0.91	0.90	0.92
5	50	100	FALSE	0.92	0.91	0.93

Any command-line input or output is written as follows:

```
h2oiris <- as.h2o(
  droplevels(iris[1:100, ]))
```

New terms and **important words** are shown in bold.

[Warnings or important notes appear in a box like this.]

[Tips and tricks appear like this.]

Reader feedback

Feedback from our readers is always welcome. Let us know what you think about this book—what you liked or disliked. Reader feedback is important for us as it helps us develop titles that you will really get the most out of.

To send us general feedback, simply e-mail feedback@packtpub.com, and mention the book's title in the subject of your message.

If there is a topic that you have expertise in and you are interested in either writing or contributing to a book, see our author guide at www.packtpub.com/authors.

Customer support

Now that you are the proud owner of a Packt book, we have a number of things to help you to get the most from your purchase.

Downloading the example code

You can download the example code files for this book from your account at http://www.packtpub.com. If you purchased this book elsewhere, you can visit http://www.packtpub.com/support and register to have the files e-mailed directly to you.

You can download the code files by following these steps:

1. Log in or register to our website using your e-mail address and password.
2. Hover the mouse pointer on the **SUPPORT** tab at the top.
3. Click on **Code Downloads & Errata**.
4. Enter the name of the book in the **Search** box.
5. Select the book for which you're looking to download the code files.
6. Choose from the drop-down menu where you purchased this book from.
7. Click on **Code Download**.

Once the file is downloaded, please make sure that you unzip or extract the folder using the latest version of:

- WinRAR / 7-Zip for Windows
- Zipeg / iZip / UnRarX for Mac
- 7-Zip / PeaZip for Linux

Downloading the color images of this book

We also provide you with a PDF file that has color images of the screenshots/ diagrams used in this book. The color images will help you better understand the changes in the output. You can download this file from https://www.packtpub.com/sites/default/files/downloads/RDeepLearningEssentials_ColorImages.pdf.

Errata

Although we have taken every care to ensure the accuracy of our content, mistakes do happen. If you find a mistake in one of our books—maybe a mistake in the text or the code—we would be grateful if you could report this to us. By doing so, you can save other readers from frustration and help us improve subsequent versions of this book. If you find any errata, please report them by visiting http://www.packtpub.com/submit-errata, selecting your book, clicking on the **Errata Submission Form** link, and entering the details of your errata. Once your errata are verified, your submission will be accepted and the errata will be uploaded to our website or added to any list of existing errata under the Errata section of that title.

To view the previously submitted errata, go to https://www.packtpub.com/books/content/support and enter the name of the book in the search field. The required information will appear under the **Errata** section.

Piracy

Piracy of copyrighted material on the Internet is an ongoing problem across all media. At Packt, we take the protection of our copyright and licenses very seriously. If you come across any illegal copies of our works in any form on the Internet, please provide us with the location address or website name immediately so that we can pursue a remedy.

Please contact us at copyright@packtpub.com with a link to the suspected pirated material.

We appreciate your help in protecting our authors and our ability to bring you valuable content.

Questions

If you have a problem with any aspect of this book, you can contact us at questions@packtpub.com, and we will do our best to address the problem.

1
Getting Started with Deep Learning

This chapter discusses deep learning, a powerful multi-layered architecture for pattern recognition, signal detection, and classification or prediction. Although deep learning is not new, it is only in the past decade that it has gained great popularity, due in part to advances in computational capacity and new ways of more efficiently training models, as well as the availability of ever-increasing amounts of data. In this chapter, you will learn what deep learning is, the R packages available for training such models, how to get your system set up for analysis, and how to connect R with **H2O**, which we will use for many of the examples and work in later chapters on how to actually train and use a deep learning model.

In this chapter, we will explore the following topics:

- What is deep learning?
- R packages that train deep learning models such as deep belief networks or deep neural networks
- Connecting R and H2O, the main package we will be using for deep learning

What is deep learning?

To understand what deep learning is, perhaps it is easiest to start with what is meant by regular machine learning. In general terms, machine learning is devoted to developing and using algorithms that learn from raw data in order to make predictions. Prediction is a very general term. For example, predictions from machine learning may include predicting how much money a customer will spend at a given company, or whether a particular credit card purchase is fraudulent. Predictions also encompass more general pattern recognition, such as what letters are present in a given image, or whether a picture is of a horse, dog, person, face, building, and so on. Deep learning is a branch of machine learning where a multi-layered (deep) architecture is used to map the relations between inputs or observed features and the outcome. This deep architecture makes deep learning particularly suitable for handling a large number of variables and allows deep learning to generate features as part of the overall learning algorithm, rather than feature creation being a separate step. Deep learning has proven particularly effective in the fields of image recognition (including handwriting as well as photo or object classification) and natural language processing, such as recognizing speech.

There are many types of machine learning algorithms. In this book, we are primarily going to focus on neural networks as these have been particularly popular in deep learning. However, this focus does not mean that it is the only technique available in machine learning or even deep learning, nor that other techniques are not valuable or even better suited, depending on the specific task. The next sections will discuss what neural networks and deep neural networks are conceptually in more depth.

Conceptual overview of neural networks

As their name suggests, neural networks draw their inspiration from neural processes and neurons in the body. Neural networks contain a series of neurons, or nodes, which are interconnected and process input. The connections between neurons are weighted, with these weights based on the function being used and learned from the data. Activation in one set of neurons and the weights (adaptively learned from the data) may then feed into other neurons, and the activation of some final neuron(s) is the **prediction**.

To make this process more concrete, an example from human visual perception may be helpful. The term **grandmother cell** is used to refer to the concept that somewhere in the brain there is a cell or neuron that responds specifically to a complex and specific object, such as your grandmother. Such specificity would require thousands of cells to represent every unique entity or object we encounter. Instead, it is thought that visual perception occurs by building up more basic pieces into complex representations. For example, the following is a picture of a square:

Figure 1.1

Rather than our visual system having cells, neurons that are activated only upon seeing the gestalt, or entirety, of a square, we can have cells that recognize horizontal and vertical lines, as shown in the following:

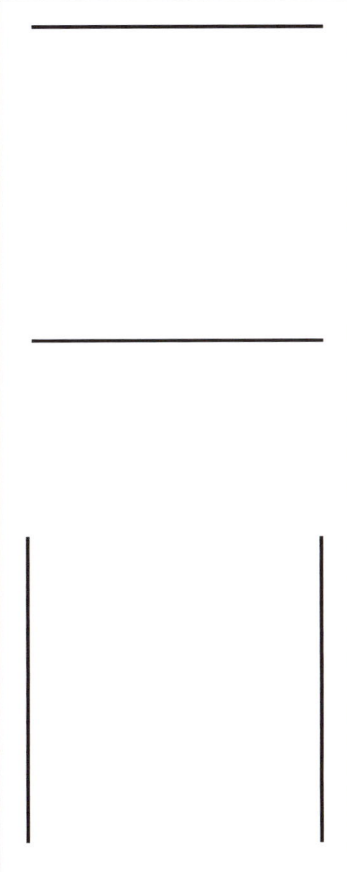

Figure 1.2

In this hypothetical case, there may be two neurons, one which is activated when it senses horizontal lines and another that is activated when it senses vertical lines. Finally, a higher-order process recognizes that it is seeing a square when both the lower order neurons are activated simultaneously.

Neural networks share some of these same concepts, with inputs being processed by a first layer of neurons that may go on to trigger another layer. Neural networks are sometimes shown as graphical models. In *Figure 1.3*, **Inputs** are data represented as squares. These may be pixels in an image, or different aspects of sounds, or something else. The next layer of **Hidden** neurons consists of neurons that recognize basic features, such as horizontal lines, vertical lines, or curved lines. Finally, the output may be a neuron that is activated by the simultaneous activation of two of the hidden neurons. In this book, observed data or features are depicted as squares, and unobserved or hidden layers as circles:

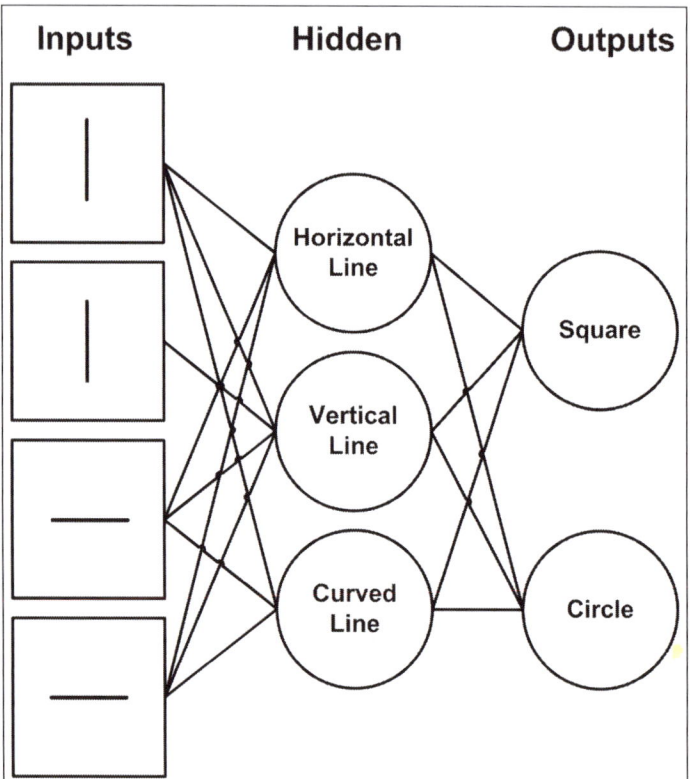

Figure 1.3

Neural networks are used to refer to a broad class of models and algorithms. Hidden neurons are generated based on some combination of the observed data, similar to a basis expansion in other statistical techniques; however, rather than choosing the form of the expansion, the weights used to create the hidden neurons are learned from the data. Neural networks can involve a variety of activation function(s), which are transformations of the weighted raw data inputs to create the hidden neurons.

A common choice for activation functions is the sigmoid function: $\sigma(x) = \dfrac{1}{1+e^{-x}}$ and the hyperbolic tangent function $f(x) = \tanh(x)$. Finally, radial basis functions are sometimes used as they are efficient function approximators. Although there are a variety of these, the Gaussian form is common: $f(x) = \exp\left(-\dfrac{\|x-c\|^2}{2\sigma^2}\right)$.

In a shallow neural network such as is shown in *Figure 1.3*, with only a single hidden layer, from the hidden units to the outputs is essentially a standard regression or classification problem. The hidden units can be denoted by h, the outputs by Y. Different outputs can be denoted by subscripts $i = 1, ..., k$ and may represent different possible classifications, such as (in our case) a circle or square. The paths from each hidden unit to each output are the weights and for the ith output are denoted by w_i. These weights are also learned from the data, just like the weights used to create the hidden layer. For classification, it is common to use a final transformation, the `softmax` function, which is $Y_i = \dfrac{e^{w_i^T h}}{\sum_i^k e^{w_i^T h}}$ as this ensures that the estimates are positive (using the exponential function) and that the probability of being in any given class sums to one. For linear regression, the `identity` function, which returns its input, is commonly used. Confusion may arise as to why there are paths between every hidden unit and output as well as every input and hidden unit. These are commonly drawn to represent that a priori any of these relations are allowed to exist. The weights must then be learned from the data, with zero or near zero weights essentially equating to dropping unnecessary relations.

This only scratches the surface of the conceptual and practical aspects of neural networks. For a slightly more in-depth introduction to neural networks, see Chapter 11 of *Hastie, T., Tibshirani, R., and Friedman, J. (2009)*, which is freely available at http://statweb.stanford.edu/~tibs/ElemStatLearn/, Chapter 16 of *Murphy, K. P. (2012)*, and Chapter 5 of *Bishop, C. M. (2006)*. Next, we will turn to a brief introduction to deep neural networks.

Deep neural networks

Perhaps the simplest, if not the most informative, definition of a **deep neural network (DNN)** is that it is a neural network with multiple hidden layers. Although a relatively simple conceptual extension of neural networks, such deep architecture provides valuable advances in terms of the capability of the models and new challenges in training them.

Using multiple hidden layers allows a more sophisticated build-up from simple elements to more complex ones. When discussing neural networks, we considered the outputs to be whether the object was a circle or a square. In a deep neural network, many circles and squares could be combined to form other more advanced shapes. One can consider two complexity aspects of a model's architecture. One is how wide or narrow it is—that is, how many neurons there are in a given layer. The second is how deep it is, or how many layers of neurons there are. For data that truly has such deep architectures, a deep neural network can fit it more accurately with fewer parameters than a **neural network (NN)**, because more layers (each with fewer neurons) can be a more efficient and accurate representation; for example, because the shallow NN cannot build more advanced shapes from basic pieces, in order to provide equal accuracy to the deep neural network it must represent each unique object. Again considering pattern recognition in images, if we are trying to train a model for text recognition the raw data may be pixels from an image. The first layer of neurons could be trained to capture different letters of the alphabet, and then another layer could recognize sets of these letters as words. The advantage is that the second layer does not have to directly learn from the pixels, which are noisy and complex. In contrast, a shallow architecture may require far more parameters, as each hidden neuron would have to be capable of going directly from pixels in an image to a complete word, and many words may overlap, creating redundancy in the model.

One of the challenges in training deep neural networks is how to efficiently learn the weights. The models are often complex and local minima abound, making the optimization problem a challenging one. One of the major advancements came in 2006, when it was shown that **Deep Belief Networks (DBNs)** could be trained one layer at a time (See *Hinton, G. E., Osindero, S., and Teh, Y. W. (2006)*). A DBN is a type of deep neural network where multiple hidden layers and connections between (but not within) layers (that is, a neuron in layer 1 may be connected to a neuron in layer 2, but may not be connected to another neuron in layer 1). This is the essentially the same definition of a **Restricted Boltzmann Machine (RBM)**—an example is shown in *Figure 1.4*—except that a RBM typically has one input layer and one hidden layer:

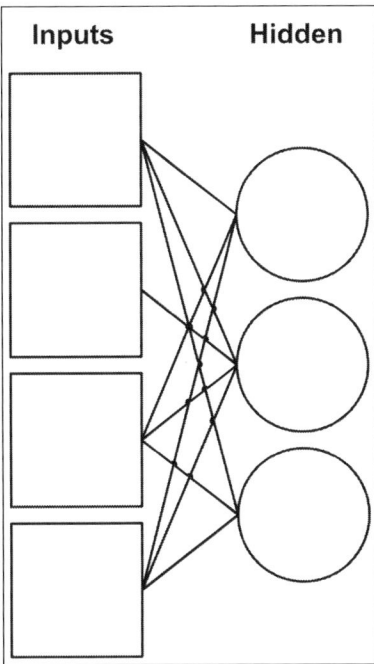

Figure 1.4

The restriction of no connections within a layer is valuable as it allows for much faster training algorithms to be used, such as the contrastive divergence algorithm. If several RBMs are stacked together, they can form a DBN. Essentially, the DBN can then be trained as a series of RBMs. The first RBM layer is trained and used to transform raw data into hidden neurons, which are then treated as a new set of inputs in a second RBM, and the process is repeated until all layers have been trained.

The benefits of the realization that DBNs could be trained one layer at a time extend beyond just DBNs, however. DBNs are sometimes used as a pre-training stage for a deep neural network. This allows the comparatively fast, greedy layer-by-layer training to be used to provide good initial estimates, which are then refined in the deep neural network using other, slower, training algorithms such as back propagation.

So far we have been primarily focused on feed-forward neural networks, where the results from one layer and neuron feed forward to the next. Before closing this section, two specific kinds of deep neural networks that have grown in popularity are worth mentioning. The first is a **Recurrent Neural Network (RNN)** where neurons send feedback signals to each other. These feedback loops allow RNNs to work well with sequences. A recent example of an application of RNNs was to automatically generate click-bait such as *One trick great hair salons don't want you to know* or *Top 10 reasons to visit Los Angeles: #6 will shock you!*. RNNs work well for such jobs as they can be seeded from a large initial pool of a few words (even just trending search terms or names) and then predict/generate what the next word should be. This process can be repeated a few times until a short phrase is generated, the click-bait. This example is drawn from a blog post by Lars Eidnes, available at `http://larseidnes.com/2015/10/13/auto-generating-clickbait-with-recurrent-neural-networks/`. The second type is a **Convolutional Neural Network (CNN)**. CNNs are most commonly used in image recognition. CNNs work by having each neuron respond to overlapping subregions of an image. The benefits of CNNs are that they require comparatively minimal pre-processing yet still do not require too many parameters through weight sharing (for example, across subregions of an image). This is particularly valuable for images as they are often not consistent. For example, imagine ten different people taking a picture of the same desk. Some may be closer or farther away or at positions resulting in essentially the same image having different heights, widths, and the amount of image captured around the focal object.

As for neural networks, this description only provides the briefest of overviews as to what deep neural networks are and some of the use cases to which they can be applied. For an overview, see *Schmidhuber, J.* (2015) as well as Chapter 28 of *Murphy, K. P.* (2012).

R packages for deep learning

Although there are a number of R packages for machine learning, there are comparatively few available for neural networks and deep learning. In this section, we will see how to install all the necessary R packages and set them up to use neural networks and deep learning.

It is helpful to have a good **integrated development environment** (IDE) for working with R and doing data analysis. I use Emacs, a powerful text editor, along with **Emacs Speaks Statistics (ESS)**, which helps Emacs work nicely with R. An easy way to get up-and-running is to use a modified distribution of Emacs designed to work nicely with R and for statistics. It is created and maintained by Vincent Goulet and is freely available at `http://vgoulet.act.ulaval.ca/en/emacs/`. Another popular R IDE is **Rstudio** (`https://www.rstudio.com/`). One advantage of both Emacs and Rstudio is that they are available on all major platforms (Windows, Mac, and Linux), so even if you switch computers you can have a consistent IDE experience.

Setting up reproducible results

Software for data science is advancing and changing rapidly. Although this is wonderful for progress, it can make reproducing someone else's results a challenge. Even your own code may not work when you go back to it a few months later. One way to address this issue is to make a record of what versions of software were used and ensure there is a snapshot of them available. For this book, we will use the R package **checkpoint** provided by Revolution Analytics; this works in connection with their server, which provides daily snapshots (checkpoints) of the **Comprehensive R Archive Network (CRAN)**. To learn more about this process, you can read the online vignette for the package available at `https://cran.r-project.org/web/packages/checkpoint/vignettes/checkpoint.html`.

This book was written using R version 3.2.3, nicknamed **Wooden Christmas-Tree**, on Windows 10 Professional x64. Although this is the latest version of R at the time of writing, as new versions are released CRAN keeps copies of older R versions both as binaries (in the future at `https://cran.r-project.org/bin/windows/base/old/`) and as source tar balls (`https://cran.r-project.org/src/base/R-3/`), which can be used to compile the source to any operating system.

For **H2O**, one of the main R packages will be used for deep learning, we will also need **Java** installed. This book was written using the Java SE Development Kit 8 update 66 for 64 bit. You can download Java for your operating system at `http://www.oracle.com/technetwork/java/javase/`.

With those steps done, we are ready to get started. To use the checkpoint package, put all your R scripts for one project together in a single folder. Installing R packages using the checkpoint package is a somewhat circular process. The checkpoint package works by scanning R scripts in the project directory to see what packages are loaded (and therefore that it needs to install), by checking for calls to the `library()` or `require()` functions. Of course, we cannot actually use the `library()` function until we have installed the packages.

To begin with, create an R script in your project directory called `checkpoint.R` with the following code:

```
## uncomment to install the checkpoint package
## install.packages("checkpoint")
library(checkpoint)

checkpoint("2016-02-20", R.version = "3.2.3")
```

Once you have created the R script, you can uncomment and run the code to install the checkpoint package. You only need to do this once, so when you are done it's best to comment the code out again so it is not re-installed each time you run the file. This is the file we will run each time we want to set up our R environment for this deep learning project. The checkpoint for this book is **20th February 2016** and we are using R version 3.2.3. Next, we can add `library()` calls for some packages we will need to be available by adding the following code to our `checkpoint.R` script (but note that these are not run yet!):

```
## Chapter 1 ##

## Tools
library(RCurl)
library(jsonlite)
library(caret)
library(e1071)

## basic stats packages
library(statmod)
library(MASS)
```

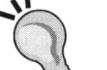

Downloading the example code

You can download the example code files for this book from your account at http://www.packtpub.com. If you purchased this book elsewhere, you can visit http://www.packtpub.com/support and register to have the files e-mailed directly to you.

You can download the code files by following these steps:

- Log in or register to our website using your e-mail address and password.
- Hover the mouse pointer on the **SUPPORT** tab at the top.
- Click on **Code Downloads & Errata**.
- Enter the name of the book in the Search box.
- Select the book for which you're looking to download the code files.
- Choose from the drop-down menu where you purchased this book from.
- Click on **Code Download**.

Once the file is downloaded, please make sure that you unzip or extract the folder using the latest version of:

- WinRAR / 7-Zip for Windows
- Zipeg / iZip / UnRarX for Mac
- 7-Zip / PeaZip for Linux

Once we have added that code, save the file so that any changes are written to the disk, and then run the first couple of lines to load the checkpoint package and the call to `checkpoint()`. The results should look something like *Figure 1.5*:

```
File  Edit  Options  Buffers  Tools  iESS  Complete  In/Out  Signals  Help

R version 3.2.3 (2015-12-10) -- "Wooden Christmas-Tree"
Copyright (C) 2015 The R Foundation for Statistical Computing
Platform: x86_64-w64-mingw32/x64 (64-bit)

R is free software and comes with ABSOLUTELY NO WARRANTY.
You are welcome to redistribute it under certain conditions.
Type 'license()' or 'licence()' for distribution details.

R is a collaborative project with many contributors.
Type 'contributors()' for more information and
'citation()' on how to cite R or R packages in publications.

Type 'demo()' for some demos, 'help()' for on-line help, or
'help.start()' for an HTML browser interface to help.
Type 'q()' to quit R.

> > options(chmhelp=FALSE, help_type="text")
> options(STERM='iESS', str.dendrogram.last="'", editor='emacsclient.exe', show.
error.locations=TRUE)
> library(checkpoint)

checkpoint: Part of the Reproducible R Toolkit from Revolution Analytics
http://projects.revolutionanalytics.com/rrt/
> checkpoint("2016-02-20", R.version = "3.2.3")
Can I create directory ~/.checkpoint for internal checkpoint use?(y/n)
y
Scanning for packages used in this project
  |============================================================| 100%
- Discovered 7 packages
Installing packages used in this project
 - Installing 'caret'
also installing the dependencies 'colorspace', 'minqa', 'nloptr', 'RcppEigen', '
RColorBrewer', 'dichromat', 'munsell', 'labeling', 'Matrix', 'lme4', 'SparseM', 
'MatrixModels', 'stringi', 'magrittr', 'digest', 'gtable', 'MASS', 'scales', 'mg
cv', 'nnet', 'pbkrtest', 'quantreg', 'codetools', 'iterators', 'Rcpp', 'stringr'
, 'lattice', 'ggplot2', 'car', 'foreach', 'plyr', 'nlme', 'reshape2'

package 'colorspace' successfully unpacked and MD5 sums checked
[ output cut ]
package 'caret' successfully unpacked and MD5 sums checked
 - Installing 'e1071'
also installing the dependency 'class'

package 'class' successfully unpacked and MD5 sums checked
package 'e1071' successfully unpacked and MD5 sums checked
 - Installing 'jsonlite'
package 'jsonlite' successfully unpacked and MD5 sums checked
 - Previously installed 'MASS'
 - Installing 'RCurl'
also installing the dependency 'bitops'

package 'bitops' successfully unpacked and MD5 sums checked
package 'RCurl' successfully unpacked and MD5 sums checked
 - Installing 'statmod'
package 'statmod' successfully unpacked and MD5 sums checked
checkpoint process complete
---
>
1\**-  *R*      All (54,2)      (iESS [R db -]: run company ElDoc)
```

Figure 1.5

The checkpoint package asks to create a directory to store specific versions of the packages used, and then finds all packages and installs them. The next sections show how to set up some specific R packages for deep learning.

Neural networks

There are several packages in R that can fit basic neural networks. The nnet package is a recommended package and can fit feed-forward neural networks with one hidden layer, like the one shown in *Figure 1.3*. For more details on the nnet package, see *Venables, W. N.* and *Ripley, B. D.* (2002). The neuralnet package also fits shallow neural networks with one hidden layer, but can train them using back-propagation and allows custom error and neuron activation functions. Finally, we come to the RSNNS package, which is an R wrapper of the **Stuttgart Neural Network Simulator (SNNS)**. The SNNS was originally written in C, but was ported to C++. RSNNS allows many types of models to fit in R. Common models are available using convenient wrappers, but the RSNNS package also makes many model components from SNNS available, making it possible to train a wide variety of models. For more details on the RSNNS package, see *Bergmeir, C.*, and *Benítez, J. M.* (2012). We will see examples of how to use these models in *Chapter 2, Training a Prediction Model*. For now, we can install them by adding the following code to the `checkpoint.R` script and saving it. Saving is important because, if our changes to the R script are not written to the disk, the `checkpoint()` function will not see the changes and will not find and install the new packages:

```
## neural networks
library(nnet)
library(neuralnet)
library(RSNNS)
```

Now, if we re-run the `checkpoint()` function and it is successful, R should tell us that it discovered eight packages and that it installed nnet, neuralnet, RSNNS, and Rcpp, a dependency for the RSNNS package.

The deepnet package

The **deepnet** package provides a number of tools for deep learning in R. Specifically, it can train RBMs and use these as part of DBNs to generate initial values to train deep neural networks. The deepnet package also allows for different activation functions, and the use of dropout for regularization. To install it, we follow the same process we used before adding the following code to the `checkpoint.R` script, saving it, and then re-running the `checkpoint()` function:

```
## deep learning
library(deepnet)
```

The darch package

The **darch** package is based on **Matlab** code by George Hinton and stands for deep architectures. It can train RBMs and DBNs along with a variety of options related to each. A limitation of the darch package is that, because it is a pure R implementation, model training tends to be slow. To install it, we follow the same process we used before adding the following code to the `checkpoint.R` script, saving it, and then re-running the `checkpoint()` function:

```
## deep learning
library(darch)
```

The H2O package

The **H2O** package provides an interface to the **H2O** software. H2O is written in Java and is fast and scalable. It provides not only deep learning functionality, but also a variety of other popular machine learning algorithms and models, and the model results can be stored as pure Java code to allow fast scoring, facilitating the deployment of models to solve real-world problems. To install it, we follow the same process we used before adding the following code to the `checkpoint.R` script, saving it, and then re-running the `checkpoint()` function:

```
## deep learning
library(h2o)
```

Connecting R and H2O

Because H2O is Java-based software with an R wrapper, to connect R to it we must initialize an instance of H2O and also connect R with it, linking or passing data and model commands to it. In this section, we will show how to get everything set up to train a model using H2O.

Initializing H2O

To initialize an H2O cluster, we use the `h2o.init()` function. Initializing a cluster will also set up a lightweight web server that allows interaction with the software via a local webpage. Generally, the `h2o.init()` function has sensible default values, but we can customize many aspects of it, and it may be particularly good to customize the number of cores/threads to use as well as how much memory we are willing for it to use, which can be accomplished as in the following code using the `max_mem_size` and `nthreads` arguments. In the code that follows, we initialize an H2O cluster to use two threads and up to three gigabytes of memory. After the code, R will indicate the location of log files, the Java version, and details about the cluster:

```
cl <- h2o.init(
  max_mem_size = "3G",
  nthreads = 2)


H2O is not running yet, starting it now...


Note:  In case of errors look at the following log files:
    C:\Users\jwile\AppData\Local\Temp\RtmpuelhZm/h2o_jwile_started_
from_r.out
    C:\Users\jwile\AppData\Local\Temp\RtmpuelhZm/h2o_jwile_started_
from_r.err


java version "1.8.0_66"
Java(TM) SE Runtime Environment (build 1.8.0_66-b18)
Java HotSpot(TM) 64-Bit Server VM (build 25.66-b18, mixed mode)


.Successfully connected to http://127.0.0.1:54321/


R is connected to the H2O cluster:
    H2O cluster uptime:          1 seconds 735 milliseconds
    H2O cluster version:         3.6.0.8
    H2O cluster name:            H2O_started_from_R_jwile_ndx127
    H2O cluster total nodes:     1
    H2O cluster total memory:    2.67 GB
    H2O cluster total cores:     4
    H2O cluster allowed cores:   2
    H2O cluster healthy:         TRUE
```

Once the cluster is initialized, we can interface with it either using R or using the web interface available at the local host (`127.0.0.1:54321`); it is shown in *Figure 1.6*:

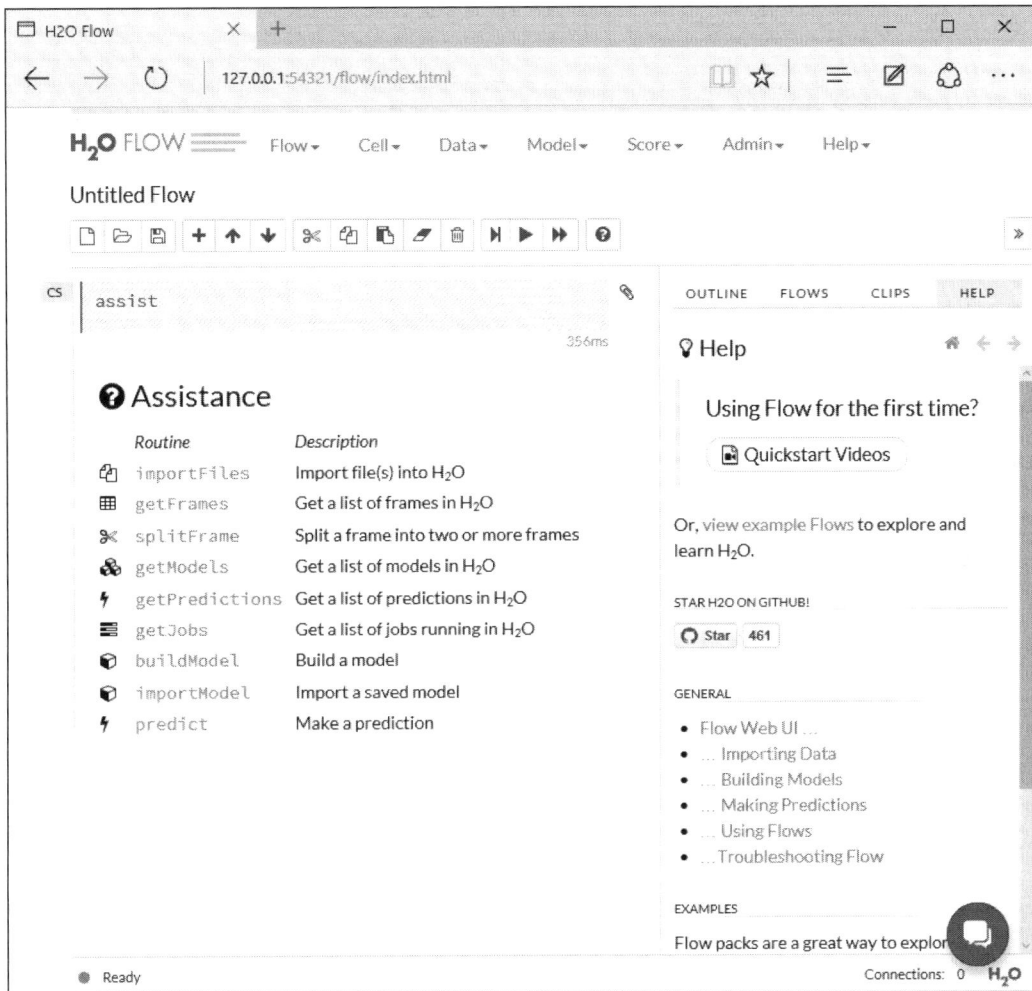

Figure 1.6

Linking datasets to an H2O cluster

There are a couple of ways to get data into an H2O cluster. If the dataset is already loaded into R, you can simply use the `as.h2o()` function as shown in the following code:

```
h2oiris <- as.h2o(
  droplevels(iris[1:100, ]))
```

We can check the results by typing the R object, h2oiris, which is simply an object that holds a reference to the H2O data. The R API queries H2O when we try to print it:

```
h2oiris
```

This returns the following output:

```
  Sepal.Length Sepal.Width Petal.Length Petal.Width Species
1          5.1         3.5          1.4         0.2  setosa
2          4.9         3.0          1.4         0.2  setosa
3          4.7         3.2          1.3         0.2  setosa
4          4.6         3.1          1.5         0.2  setosa
5          5.0         3.6          1.4         0.2  setosa
6          5.4         3.9          1.7         0.4  setosa


[100 rows x 5 columns]
```

We can also check the levels of factor variables, such as the Species variable, as shown in the following:

```
h2o.levels(h2oiris, 5)
[1] setosa     versicolor
```

In real-world uses, it is more likely that the data already exists somewhere; rather than load the data into R only to export it into H2O (a costly operation as it creates an unnecessary copy of the data in R), we can just load data directly into H2O. First we will create a CSV file based on the built-in mtcars dataset, then we will tell the H2O instance to read the data using R. Printing again shows the data:

```
write.csv(mtcars, file = "mtcars.csv")


h2omtcars <- h2o.importFile(
   path = "mtcars.csv")


h2omtcars
                 C1  mpg cyl disp  hp drat    wt  qsec vs am gear carb
1      Mazda RX4 21.0   6  160 110 3.90 2.620 16.46  0  1    4    4
2  Mazda RX4 Wag 21.0   6  160 110 3.90 2.875 17.02  0  1    4    4
3     Datsun 710 22.8   4  108  93 3.85 2.320 18.61  1  1    4    1
4  Hornet 4 Drive 21.4   6  258 110 3.08 3.215 19.44  1  0    3    1
```

```
5 Hornet Sportabout 18.7   8   360 175 3.15 3.440 17.02  0  0    3    2
6               Valiant 18.1   6   225 105 2.76 3.460 20.22  1  0    3    1
[32 rows x 12 columns]
```

Finally, the data need not be located on the local disk. We can also ask H2O to read in data from a URL as shown in this last example, which uses a dataset made available from the UCLA Statistical Consulting Group:

```
h2obin <- h2o.importFile(
    path = "http://www.ats.ucla.edu/stat/data/binary.csv")


h2obin
   admit gre  gpa rank
1      0 380 3.61    3
2      1 660 3.67    3
3      1 800 4.00    1
4      1 640 3.19    4
5      0 520 2.93    4
6      1 760 3.00    2


[400 rows x 4 columns]
```

Summary

This chapter presented a brief introduction to NNs and deep neural networks. Using multiple hidden layers, deep neural networks have been a revolution in machine learning by providing a powerful unsupervised learning and feature extraction component that can be standalone or integrated as part of a supervised model.

There are many applications of such models, and they are being increasingly used by large companies such as Google, Microsoft, and Facebook. Examples of tasks for deep learning are image recognition (for example, automatically tagging faces, or identifying keywords for an image), voice recognition, and text translation (for example, to go from English to Spanish, or vice versa). Work is even being done on text recognition such as sentiment analysis to try to identify whether a sentence or paragraph is generally positive or negative, particularly useful for evaluating perceptions about a product or service. Imagine being able to scrape reviews and social media for any mention of your product and being able to analyse whether it was being discussed more or less favourably than the month or year before!

This chapter also showed how to set up R and the necessary software and packages installed, in a reproducible way to match the versions used in this book.

In the next chapter, we will begin to train neural networks and generate our own predictions.

2
Training a Prediction Model

This chapter shows how to build and train basic neural networks in R through hands-on examples that also emphasize the importance of evaluating different tuning parameters for models to find the best set. Although evaluating a variety of tuning parameters can help increase the performance of a model, it can also lead to overfitting, the next topic covered in the chapter. The chapter closes with an example use case classifying activity data from a smartphone as walking, going up or down stairs, sitting, standing, or lying down.

This chapter covers the following topics:

- Neural networks in R
- The problem of overfitting data – the consequences explained
- Use case – build and apply a neural network

Neural networks in R

To train basic (that is, "shallow" with a single hidden layer) neural networks in R, we will use the **nnet** and the **RSNNS** (*Bergmeir, C., and Benítez, J. M.* (2012)) packages. From the previous chapter, these should already be installed and based on a **20th February 2016** checkpoint so our results are fully reproducible. Although it is possible to interface with the nnet package directly, we are going to use it through the **caret** package, which is short for **Classification and Regression Training**. The caret package provides a standardized interface to work with many machine learning models in R (Kuhn, 2008; Kuhn and Johnson, 2013), and also has some useful features for validation and performance assessment that we will use in this chapter and the next.

For our first examples of building neural networks, we will use a classic classification problem—recognizing handwritten digits based on pictures. The data can be downloaded from `https://www.kaggle.com/c/digit-recognizer` and comes in an easy-to-use CSV format, where each column of the dataset, or feature, represents a pixel from the image. Each image has been normalized to a fixed size so every image has the same number of pixels. The first column contains the actual digit label, and the remaining are pixel darkness values, to be used for classification. The downloaded files, called `train.csv` and `test.csv`, were placed in the same folder as the R scripts, so they can easily be read in. If you put them in different folders, just change the paths accordingly.

Building a neural network

To get started, we will first load our packages, by calling `source()` on the script where we loaded them, and set the checkpoint for the versions to use. Then we can read in the training data downloaded from **Kaggle**, and take a quick look at what it is like:

```
source("checkpoint.R")

## output omitted

digits.train <- read.csv("train.csv")


dim(digits.train)


[1] 42000    785


head(colnames(digits.train), 4)


[1] "label"  "pixel0" "pixel1" "pixel2"


tail(colnames(digits.train), 4)


[1] "pixel780" "pixel781" "pixel782" "pixel783"


head(digits.train[, 1:4])
```

```
  label pixel0 pixel1 pixel2
1     1      0      0      0
2     0      0      0      0
3     1      0      0      0
```

4	4	0	0	0
5	0	0	0	0
6	0	0	0	0

We will convert the labels (the digits 0 to 9) to a factor so R knows that this is a classification not a regression problem. If this were a real-world problem, we would want to use all 42,000 observations but, for the sake of reducing how long it takes to run, we will select just the first 5,000 for these first examples of building and training a neural network. We also separate the data into the features or predictors (`digits.X`) and the outcome (`digits.Y`). We are using all the columns except the labels as the predictors here:

```
## convert to factor
digits.train$label <- factor(digits.train$label, levels = 0:9)
i <- 1:5000
digits.X <- digits.train[i, -1]
digits.y <- digits.train[i, 1]
```

Finally, before we get started building our neural network, let's quickly check the distribution of the digits. This can be important as, for example, if one digit occurs very rarely, we may need to adjust our modeling approach to ensure that, even though it is rare, it is given enough weight in performance evaluation if we care about accurately predicting that digit as well. The following code snippet creates a bar plot showing the frequency of each digit label (*Figure 2.1*). They are fairly evenly distributed so there is no real need to increase the weight or importance given to any particular one:

```
barplot(table(digits.y))
```

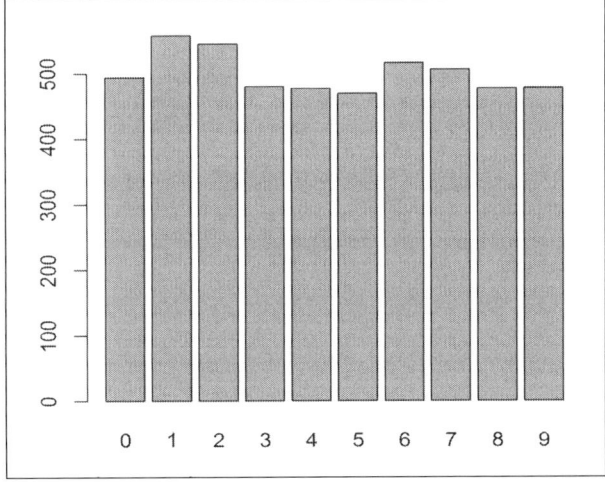

Figure 2.1

Now let's build and train our first neural network using the nnet package through the caret package wrapper. First, we use the `set.seed()` function and specify a specific seed so that the results are reproducible. The exact seed is not important. This same approach is also used in later examples repeating the same seed, because what matters is that the same seed is used for the same model, not whether different models have different or similar seeds. The `train()` function first takes the feature or predictor data, the x argument, and then the outcome variable, the y argument. The `train()` function can work with a variety of models, determined via the `method` argument. Although many aspects of machine learning models are learned automatically, some parameters have to be set. These vary by the method used; for example, in neural networks one parameter is the number of hidden units. The `train()` function provides an easy way to try a variety of these tuning parameters as a named data frame to the `tuneGrid` argument. It returns the performance measures for each set of tuning parameters and returns the best trained model. We will start with just five hidden neurons in our model, and a modest decay rate, sometimes also called the **learning rate**. The learning rate controls how much each iteration or step can influence the current weights. Another argument, `trControl`, controls additional aspects of `train()`, and is used, when a variety of tuning parameters are being evaluated, to tell the caret package how to validate and pick the best tuning parameter.

For this example, we will set the method for training control to `"none"` as we only have one set of tuning parameters being used here. Finally, at the end we can specify additional, named arguments that are passed on to the actual `nnet()` function (or whatever algorithm is specified). Because of the number of predictors (784), we increase the maximum number of weights to 10,000 and specify a maximum of 100 iterations. Due to the relatively small amount of data, and the paucity of hidden neurons, this first model does not take too long to run:

```
set.seed(1234)

digits.m1 <- train(x = digits.X, y = digits.y,
          method = "nnet",
          tuneGrid = expand.grid(
            .size = c(5),
            .decay = 0.1),
          trControl = trainControl(method = "none"),
          MaxNWts = 10000,
          maxit = 100)
```

The `predict()` function generates a set of predictions for data. When called on the results of a model without specifying any new data, it just generates predictions on the same data used for training. After calculating and storing the predicted digits, we can examine their distribution, shown in *Figure 2.2*. Even before looking at the performance measures for this first model, given the actual distribution (*Figure 2.1*) it is clear this model is not optimal:

```
digits.yhat1 <- predict(digits.m1)
barplot(table(digits.yhat1))
```

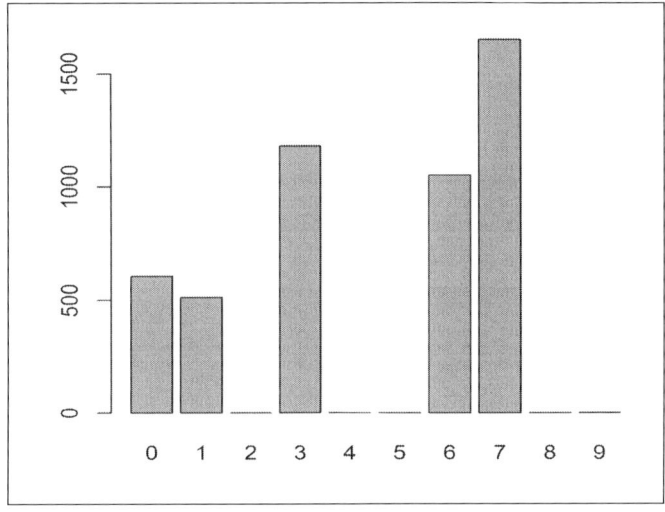

Figure 2.2

Graphically examining the distribution is just a simple check of the predictions. A more formal evaluation of model performance is possible using the `confusionMatrix()` function in the caret package. Because there is a function by the same name in the RSNNS package, they are masked so we use the special `caret::` code to tell R which version of the function to use. The input is simply a frequency cross tab between the actual digits and the predicted digits. The remaining performance metrics are calculated from these.

Because we had multiple digits, there are three main sections to the performance output. First, the actual frequency cross tab is shown. Correct predictions are on the diagonal, with various frequencies of misclassification on the off diagonals. Next are the overall statistics, which refer to the model performance across all classes. Accuracy is simply the proportion of cases correctly classified, along with a 95% confidence interval, which can be useful especially for smaller datasets where there may be considerable uncertainty in the estimate. The `No Information Rate` refers to what accuracy could be expected without any information by merely guessing the most frequent class, in this case, *1*, which occurred 11.16% of the time. The p-value tests whether the observed accuracy (44.3%) is significantly different than the `No Information Rate` (11.2%). Although statistically significant, this is not very meaningful for digit classification where we would expect to do far better than simply guessing the most frequent digit! Finally, individual performance metrics for each digit are shown. These are based on calculating that digit versus every other digit, so that each is a binary comparison. The following 2 x 2 table contains all the information needed to calculate the various measures, and the formulae for all the measures are shown here:

	Positive	Negative
Predicted positive	True positive (TP)	False positive (FP)
Predicted negative	False negative (FN)	True negative (TN)

$$Sensitivity = \frac{TP}{TP + FN}$$

$$Specificity = \frac{TN}{TN + FP}$$

$$Positive\ Predictive\ Value\ (PPV) = \frac{TP}{TP + FP}$$

$$Negative\ Predictive\ Value\ (NPV) = \frac{TN}{FN + TN}$$

$$Detection\ Rate = \frac{TP}{TP + FN + FP + TN}$$

$$Detection\ Prevalence = \frac{TP + FP}{TP + FN + FP + TN}$$

For example, the sensitivity for digit 0 can be interpreted as meaning that 78.5% of zero digits were captured or correctly predicted to be zeroes. The specificity for digit 0 can be interpreted as meaning that 95.2% of cases that were predicted to be a digit other than zero were not zero. The detection rate is just the percentage of true positives, and finally the detection prevalence is the proportion of cases predicted to be positive, regardless of whether they actually are or not. The balanced accuracy is the mean of the sensitivity and specificity. The remaining columns present the same information for each of the remaining digits:

```
caret::confusionMatrix(xtabs(~digits.yhat1 + digits.y))
```

Confusion Matrix and Statistics

```
             digits.y
digits.yhat1    0    1    2    3    4    5    6    7    8    9
           0  388    2   40   41    7   75   23    4   23    2
           1    0  495    3    0    0    3    0    4    3    4
           2    0    0    0    0    0    0    0    0    0    0
           3   51   30   36  379    6  329    3   18  290   38
           4    0    0    0    0    0    0    0    0    0    0
           5    0    0    0    0    0    0    0    0    0    0
           6   44    5  304    9  131   29  484    9   16   19
           7   11   26  162   51  333   33    6  470  145  415
           8    0    0    0    0    0    0    0    0    0    0
           9    0    0    0    0    0    0    0    1    0    0
```

Overall Statistics

```
                Accuracy : 0.4432
                  95% CI : (0.4294, 0.4571)
     No Information Rate : 0.1116
     P-Value [Acc > NIR] : < 2.2e-16

                   Kappa : 0.3805
  Mcnemar's Test P-Value : NA
```

Statistics by Class:

	Class: 0	Class: 1	Class: 2	Class: 3	Class: 4
Sensitivity	0.7854	0.8871	0.000	0.7896	0.0000
Specificity	0.9518	0.9962	1.000	0.8228	1.0000
Pos Pred Value	0.6413	0.9668	NaN	0.3212	NaN
Neg Pred Value	0.9759	0.9860	0.891	0.9736	0.9046
Prevalence	0.0988	0.1116	0.109	0.0960	0.0954
Detection Rate	0.0776	0.0990	0.000	0.0758	0.0000
Detection Prevalence	0.1210	0.1024	0.000	0.2360	0.0000
Balanced Accuracy	0.8686	0.9416	0.500	0.8062	0.5000

	Class: 5	Class: 6	Class: 7	Class: 8	Class: 9
Sensitivity	0.0000	0.9380	0.9289	0.0000	0.0000
Specificity	1.0000	0.8738	0.7370	1.0000	0.9998
Pos Pred Value	NaN	0.4610	0.2845	NaN	0.0000
Neg Pred Value	0.9062	0.9919	0.9892	0.9046	0.9044
Prevalence	0.0938	0.1032	0.1012	0.0954	0.0956
Detection Rate	0.0000	0.0968	0.0940	0.0000	0.0000
Detection Prevalence	0.0000	0.2100	0.3304	0.0000	0.0002
Balanced Accuracy	0.5000	0.9059	0.8329	0.5000	0.4999

Now that we have some basic understanding of how to set up, train, and evaluate model performance, we will try a few different models, increasing the number of hidden neurons, which is one key way to improve model performance, at the cost of greatly increasing the model complexity. Recall from *Chapter 1*, *Getting Started with Deep Learning*, that every predictor or feature connects to each hidden neuron, and each hidden neuron connects to each outcome or output. With 784 features, each additional hidden neuron adds a substantial number of parameters, which also results in longer run times. Depending on your computer, be prepared to wait a number of minutes for these next models to finish:

```
set.seed(1234)

digits.m2 <- train(digits.X, digits.y,
          method = "nnet",
          tuneGrid = expand.grid(
            .size = c(10),
            .decay = 0.1),
          trControl = trainControl(method = "none"),
           MaxNWts = 50000,
           maxit = 100)


digits.yhat2 <- predict(digits.m2)
barplot(table(digits.yhat2))
```

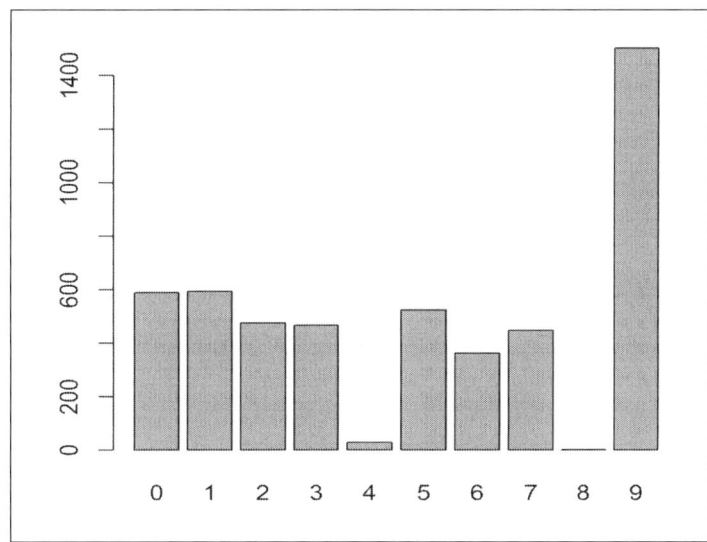

Figure 2.3

```
caret::confusionMatrix(xtabs(~digits.yhat2 + digits.y))
```

Confusion Matrix and Statistics

```
          digits.y
digits.yhat2   0    1    2    3    4    5    6    7    8    9
          0  395    0   14   23    0  120    6   12   15    5
          1    2  518   35   10    0    7    0   10    8    4
          2   23   23  323   15    8   37   30    1   15    2
          3    0    4   24  337    0   49    0   12   37    5
          4    3    0    0    0   10   14    2    0    0    0
          5   44    0   20   60    0  146   10    1  235    9
          6    1    1   25    2    0    3  327    0    3    0
          7    3    1    7    3    3   11    7  392    3   19
          8    0    0    0    0    0    0    1    0    0    0
          9   23   11   97   30  456   82  133   78  161  434
```

Overall Statistics

```
               Accuracy : 0.5764
                 95% CI : (0.5626, 0.5901)
    No Information Rate : 0.1116
    P-Value [Acc > NIR] : < 2.2e-16

                  Kappa : 0.5293
 Mcnemar's Test P-Value : NA
```

Statistics by Class:

```
                Class: 0 Class: 1 Class: 2 Class: 3 Class: 4
Sensitivity       0.7996   0.9283   0.5927   0.7021  0.02096
```

Specificity	0.9567	0.9829	0.9654	0.9710	0.99580
Pos Pred Value	0.6695	0.8721	0.6771	0.7201	0.34483
Neg Pred Value	0.9776	0.9909	0.9509	0.9684	0.90606
Prevalence	0.0988	0.1116	0.1090	0.0960	0.09540
Detection Rate	0.0790	0.1036	0.0646	0.0674	0.00200
Detection Prevalence	0.1180	0.1188	0.0954	0.0936	0.00580
Balanced Accuracy	0.8782	0.9556	0.7790	0.8366	0.50838

	Class: 5	Class: 6	Class: 7	Class: 8	Class: 9
Sensitivity	0.3113	0.6337	0.7747	0.0000	0.9079
Specificity	0.9164	0.9922	0.9873	0.9998	0.7632
Pos Pred Value	0.2781	0.9033	0.8731	0.0000	0.2884
Neg Pred Value	0.9278	0.9592	0.9750	0.9046	0.9874
Prevalence	0.0938	0.1032	0.1012	0.0954	0.0956
Detection Rate	0.0292	0.0654	0.0784	0.0000	0.0868
Detection Prevalence	0.1050	0.0724	0.0898	0.0002	0.3010
Balanced Accuracy	0.6138	0.8130	0.8810	0.4999	0.8356

Increasing from 5 to 10 hidden neurons improved our in-sample performance from an overall accuracy of 44.3% to 57.6%, but this is still quite some way from ideal (imagine character recognition software that mixed up 42.4% of all the characters!). We increase again, this time to 40 hidden neurons, and wait even longer for the model to finish training:

```
set.seed(1234)
digits.m3 <- train(digits.X, digits.y,
          method = "nnet",
          tuneGrid = expand.grid(
             .size = c(40),
             .decay = 0.1),
          trControl = trainControl(method = "none"),
          MaxNWts = 50000,
          maxit = 100)
```

```
digits.yhat3 <- predict(digits.m3)
barplot(table(digits.yhat3))
```

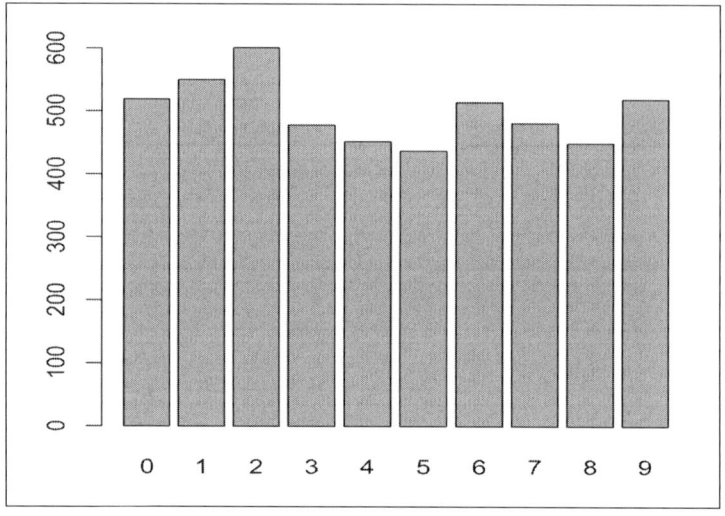

Figure 2.4

```
caret::confusionMatrix(xtabs(~digits.yhat3 + digits.y))
```

Confusion Matrix and Statistics

```
             digits.y
digits.yhat3   0    1    2    3    4    5    6    7    8    9
           0 461    0    7    3    0   20   16    2    3    7
           1   0  521    3    4    0    2    2    6   10    2
           2  17    3  469   30    2   13   16   10   39    2
           3   1    5   11  352    2   43    2    9   48    5
           4   1    0    6    1  394    7    0    4    3   36
           5   3    4    2   23    1  334   12    1   51    6
           6   6    1   19    3   15   10  455    1    3    1
           7   0    2    8    7    5    5    2  411    6   35
           8   2   20   10   46    4   28    9   10  297   23
           9   3    2   10   11   54    7    2   52   17  361
```

```
Overall Statistics

                 Accuracy : 0.811
                   95% CI : (0.7999, 0.8218)
      No Information Rate : 0.1116
      P-Value [Acc > NIR] : < 2.2e-16


                    Kappa : 0.7899
    Mcnemar's Test P-Value : NA


Statistics by Class:
```

	Class: 0	Class: 1	Class: 2	Class: 3	Class: 4
Sensitivity	0.9332	0.9337	0.8606	0.7333	0.8260
Specificity	0.9871	0.9935	0.9704	0.9721	0.9872
Pos Pred Value	0.8882	0.9473	0.7804	0.7364	0.8717
Neg Pred Value	0.9926	0.9917	0.9827	0.9717	0.9818
Prevalence	0.0988	0.1116	0.1090	0.0960	0.0954
Detection Rate	0.0922	0.1042	0.0938	0.0704	0.0788
Detection Prevalence	0.1038	0.1100	0.1202	0.0956	0.0904
Balanced Accuracy	0.9602	0.9636	0.9155	0.8527	0.9066

	Class: 5	Class: 6	Class: 7	Class: 8	Class: 9
Sensitivity	0.7122	0.8818	0.8123	0.6226	0.7552
Specificity	0.9773	0.9868	0.9844	0.9664	0.9651
Pos Pred Value	0.7643	0.8852	0.8545	0.6615	0.6956
Neg Pred Value	0.9704	0.9864	0.9790	0.9604	0.9739
Prevalence	0.0938	0.1032	0.1012	0.0954	0.0956
Detection Rate	0.0668	0.0910	0.0822	0.0594	0.0722
Detection Prevalence	0.0874	0.1028	0.0962	0.0898	0.1038
Balanced Accuracy	0.8447	0.9343	0.8983	0.7945	0.8601

Using 40 hidden neurons has improved performance dramatically again, up to 81.1% overall. Model performance for 3s, 5s, 8s, and 9s is still not great, but the remaining digits are quite good. If this were a real research or business problem, we might continue trying additional neurons, tuning the decay rate, or modifying features in order to try to boost model performance further, but for now we will move on.

Next, we will take a look at how to train neural networks using the RSNNS package. This package provides an interface to quite a variety of possible models using the **Stuttgart Neural Network Simulator (SNNS)** code; however, for a basic, single-hidden-layer, feed-forward neural network, we can use the `mlp()` convenience wrapper function, which stands for multi-layer perceptron. The RSNNS package is a bit more finicky to use than the convenience of nnet via the caret package, but one benefit is that it can be far more flexible and allows for many other types of neural network architectures to be trained, including recurrent neural networks, and also has a greater variety of learning functions.

One difference between the nnet and RSNNS package is that for multi-class outcomes (such as digits), RSNNS requires a dummy coded matrix, so each possible class is represented as a column coded as 0/1. This is facilitated using the `decodeClassLabels()` function, and a bit of the output is shown next:

```
head(decodeClassLabels(digits.y))
```

```
      0 1 2 3 4 5 6 7 8 9
[1,]  0 1 0 0 0 0 0 0 0 0
[2,]  1 0 0 0 0 0 0 0 0 0
[3,]  0 1 0 0 0 0 0 0 0 0
[4,]  0 0 0 0 1 0 0 0 0 0
[5,]  1 0 0 0 0 0 0 0 0 0
[6,]  1 0 0 0 0 0 0 0 0 0
```

Since we had reasonably good success with 40 hidden neurons, we will use the same size here. Rather than standard propagation as the learning function, we will use resilient propagation, based on the classic work of *Riedmiller, M.*, and *Braun, H.* (1993). Note also that, because a matrix of outcomes is passed, although the predicted probability will not exceed 1 for any single digit, the sum of predicted probabilities across all digits may exceed 1 and also may be less than 1 (that is, for some cases, the model may not predict they are very likely to represent any of the digits). As before, we can get in-sample predictions, but here we have to use another function, `fitted.values()`. Because this again returns a matrix where each column represents a single digit, we use the `encodeClassLabels()` function to convert back into a single vector of digit labels to plot (*Figure 2.5*) and evaluate model performance:

```
set.seed(1234)

digits.m4 <- mlp(as.matrix(digits.X),
                 decodeClassLabels(digits.y),
                 size = 40,
```

```
            learnFunc = "Rprop",
            shufflePatterns = FALSE,
            maxit = 60)
digits.yhat4 <- fitted.values(digits.m4)
digits.yhat4 <- encodeClassLabels(digits.yhat4)
barplot(table(digits.yhat4))
```

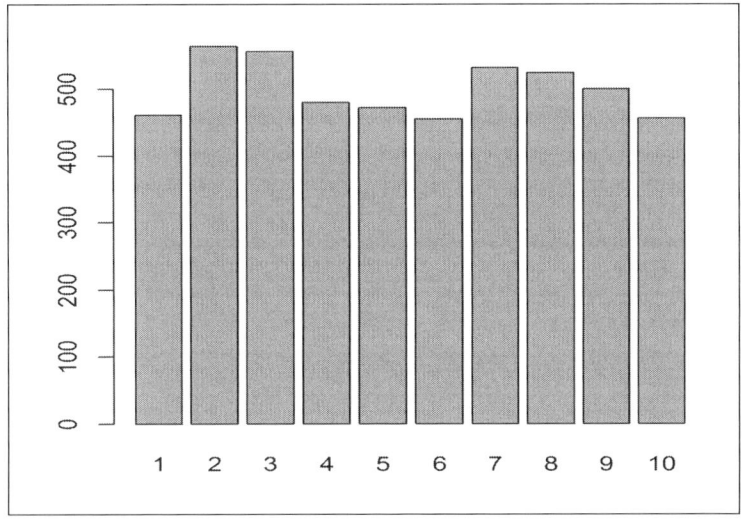

Figure 2.5

Once we have the predicted probabilities, evaluating model performance is virtually the same as when using the nnet and caret packages. The only catch is that, when the output is encoded back into a single vector, by default the digits are labeled 1 to k, where k is the number of classes. Because the digits are 0 to 9, to make them match the original digit vector, we subtract 1. Next we can see that, using the learning algorithms from the RSNNS package, we obtained a somewhat higher performance with the same number of hidden neurons. Next we turn to generating predictions for out-of-sample data:

```
caret::confusionMatrix(xtabs(~ I(digits.yhat4 - 1) + digits.y))


Confusion Matrix and Statistics

                  digits.y
I(digits.yhat4 - 1)   0   1   2   3   4   5   6   7   8   9
                  0 451   0   0   1   0   2   3   2   1   1
```

```
1   0 534   4   2   3   1   0   7  11   2
2   6   3 496  17   3   4   2   4  20   1
3   9   5  11 406   3  21   0   2  13  10
4   2   1   6   0 415   7   4   4   9  24
5  12   2   0  14   3 376   8   4  23  13
6   4   4   2   2   3  12 493   2   9   1
7   3   0  10   7   4   1   1 460   1  37
8   5   9  14  28  12  31   5   8 375  13
9   2   0   2   3  31  14   0  13  15 376
```

Overall Statistics

```
              Accuracy : 0.8764
                95% CI : (0.867, 0.8854)
    No Information Rate : 0.1116
    P-Value [Acc > NIR] : < 2.2e-16

                 Kappa : 0.8626
 Mcnemar's Test P-Value : NA
```

Statistics by Class:

	Class: 0	Class: 1	Class: 2	Class: 3	Class: 4
Sensitivity	0.9130	0.9570	0.9101	0.8458	0.8700
Specificity	0.9978	0.9932	0.9865	0.9836	0.9874
Pos Pred Value	0.9783	0.9468	0.8921	0.8458	0.8792
Neg Pred Value	0.9905	0.9946	0.9890	0.9836	0.9863
Prevalence	0.0988	0.1116	0.1090	0.0960	0.0954
Detection Rate	0.0902	0.1068	0.0992	0.0812	0.0830
Detection Prevalence	0.0922	0.1128	0.1112	0.0960	0.0944
Balanced Accuracy	0.9554	0.9751	0.9483	0.9147	0.9287

	Class: 5	Class: 6	Class: 7	Class: 8	Class: 9
Sensitivity	0.8017	0.9554	0.9091	0.7862	0.7866
Specificity	0.9826	0.9913	0.9858	0.9724	0.9823
Pos Pred Value	0.8264	0.9267	0.8779	0.7500	0.8246
Neg Pred Value	0.9795	0.9949	0.9897	0.9773	0.9776

Prevalence	0.0938	0.1032	0.1012	0.0954	0.0956
Detection Rate	0.0752	0.0986	0.0920	0.0750	0.0752
Detection Prevalence	0.0910	0.1064	0.1048	0.1000	0.0912
Balanced Accuracy	0.8921	0.9734	0.9474	0.8793	0.8845

Generating predictions from a neural network

Up until now, we have only generated in-sample predictions on the same data used to train the neural network, and we have accepted all the defaults for obtaining the classifications. However, there are actually several options, even once the model is trained. For any given observation, there can be a probability of membership in any of a number of classes (for example, an observation may have a 40% chance of being a "5", a 20% chance of being a "6", and so on). For evaluating the performance of the model, some choices have to be made about how to go from the probability of class membership to a discrete classification. In this section, we will explore a few of these options in more detail, and also take a look at generating predictions on data not used for training.

So long as there are no perfect ties, the simplest method may be to classify observations based on the high predicted probability. Another approach, which the RSNNS package calls the **winner takes all (WTA)** method, is to choose the class with the highest probability so long as there are no ties, the highest probability is above a user-defined threshold (the threshold could be zero), and the remaining classes all have a predicted probability under the maximum minus another user-defined threshold. Otherwise, observations are classified as unknown. If both thresholds are zero (the default), this equates to saying that there must be one unique maximum. The advantage of such an approach is that it provides some quality control. In the digit classification example we have been exploring, there are 10 possible classes. Suppose nine of the digits had a predicted probability of 0.099, and the remaining class had a predicted probability of 0.109. Although one class is technically more likely than the others, the difference is fairly trivial and we may conclude that the model cannot with any certainty classify that observation. A final method, called 402040, classifies if only one value is above a user-defined threshold, and all other values are below another user-defined threshold; if multiple values are above the first threshold, or any value is not below the second threshold, it treats the observation as unknown. Again, the goal here is to provide some quality control. It may seem like this is unnecessary because uncertainty in predictions should come out in the model performance. However, it can be helpful to know if your model was highly certain in its prediction and right or wrong, or uncertain and right or wrong.

Finally, in some cases not all classes are equally important. For example, in a medical context where a variety of biomarkers and genes are collected on patients and used to classify whether they are healthy or not, at risk of cancer, or at risk of heart disease, even a 40% chance of having cancer may be enough to warrant further investigation, even if they have a 60% chance of being healthy. This has to do with the performance measures we saw earlier where, beyond overall accuracy, we can assess aspects such as sensitivity, specificity, and positive and negative predictive values. There are cases where overall accuracy is less important than making sure no one is missed.

The following code shows the raw probabilities for the in-sample data, and the impact these different choices have on the predicted values:

```
digits.yhat4.insample <- fitted.values(digits.m4)
head(round(digits.yhat4.insample, 2))
```

```
       [,1] [,2] [,3] [,4] [,5] [,6] [,7] [,8] [,9] [,10]
[1,]  0.00 0.89 0.00 0.01 0.00 0.00 0.00 0.00 0.21     0
[2,]  0.99 0.00 0.00 0.02 0.00 0.00 0.00 0.01 0.00     0
[3,]  0.00 1.00 0.09 0.00 0.00 0.00 0.00 0.05 0.00     0
[4,]  0.00 0.00 0.00 0.00 0.22 0.00 0.02 0.05 0.00     0
[5,]  1.00 0.00 0.02 0.00 0.00 0.00 0.00 0.00 0.00     0
[6,]  0.99 0.00 0.00 0.00 0.00 0.06 0.00 0.00 0.00     0
```

```
table(encodeClassLabels(digits.yhat4.insample,
                   method = "WTA", l = 0, h = 0))
```

```
  1   2   3   4   5   6   7   8   9  10
461 564 556 480 472 455 532 524 500 456
```

```
table(encodeClassLabels(digits.yhat4.insample,
                   method = "WTA", l = 0, h = .5))
```

```
  0   1   2   3   4   5   6   7   8   9  10
569 448 544 497 400 429 366 499 463 379 406
```

```
table(encodeClassLabels(digits.yhat4.insample,
```

```
                     method = "WTA", l = .2, h = .5))
```

```
  0    1    2    3    4    5    6    7    8    9   10
658  443  542  490  393  408  358  493  460  364  391
```

```
table(encodeClassLabels(digits.yhat4.insample,
                    method = "402040", l = .4, h = .6))
```

```
  0    1    2    3    4    5    6    7    8    9   10
907  431  526  472  363  383  326  475  448  301  368
```

We can easily generate predicted values for new data using the `predict()` function. For this, we will use the next 5,000 observations. Note that even generating these predictions took a couple of minutes on a new desktop:

```
i2 <- 5001:10000
digits.yhat4.pred <- predict(digits.m4,
                         as.matrix(digits.train[i2, -1]))
```

```
table(encodeClassLabels(digits.yhat4.pred,
                    method = "WTA", l = 0, h = 0))
```

```
  1    2    3    4    5    6    7    8    9   10
449  570  531  518  476  442  522  533  468  491
```

Having generated predictions on out-of-sample data (that is, data that was not used to train the model), we can now proceed to examine problems related to overfitting the data and the impact on the evaluation of model performance.

The problem of overfitting data – the consequences explained

A common issue in machine learning is the problem of overfitting data. Generally, overfitting is used to refer to the phenomenon where, in the data used to train the model, the model performs better than it does on data not used to train the model (holdout data, future real use, and so on). Overfitting occurs when a model fits what is essentially noise in the training data. It appears to become more accurate as it accounts for the noise, but because the noise changes from one dataset to the next, this accuracy does not apply to any data but the training data—it does not generalize.

Overfitting can occur at any time but tends to become more severe as the ratio of parameters to information increases. Usually, this is can be thought of as the ratio of parameters to observations, but not always (for example, suppose the outcome is a rare event that occurs in 1 in 5 million people, a sample size of 15 million may still only have 3 people experiencing the event and would not support a complex model at all—information is low even though the sample size is large). To consider a simple but extreme case, imagine fitting a straight line to two data points. The fit will be perfect, and in those two training data your linear regression model will appear to have fully accounted for all variations in the data. However, if we then applied that line to another 1,000 cases, we might not expect it to fit very well at all.

In the previous section, we generated out-of-sample predictions for the RSNNS model we trained. We know that, in-sample, the accuracy was 87.6%. How good is that estimate? We can examine how well the model generalizes by checking the accuracy on the out-of-sample predictions using code that is by now quite familiar. Next we can see that it is still doing fairly well, but the accuracy is reduced to 83.6% on the holdout data. Here there appears to have been approximately a 4% loss; or, put differently, using training data to evaluate model performance resulted in an overly optimistic estimate of the accuracy, and that overestimate was 4%:

```
caret::confusionMatrix(xtabs(~digits.train[i2, 1] +
  I(encodeClassLabels(digits.yhat4.pred) - 1)))
Confusion Matrix and Statistics

                   I(encodeClassLabels(digits.yhat4.pred) - 1)
digits.train[i2, 1]   0   1   2   3   4   5   6   7   8   9
                  0 429   0  13  16   4   9   8   4   9   5
                  1   0 515   9   3   0   2   2   2   4   0
                  2   4   7 427  17   2   3  12  10  12   6
                  3   0   2  20 416   2  28   5  11  40   5
                  4   0   6   6   8 392   7  13   2  19  37
                  5   8   2   4  24  15 335  11   7  21  10
                  6   2   1   8   1   1   9 460   0   3   2
                  7   1  14  22   9   8   2   2 459   3  13
                  8   4  23  19  11  16  27   8   5 348  12
                  9   1   0   3  13  36  20   1  33   9 401
```

Overall Statistics

```
            Accuracy : 0.836
              95% CI : (0.826, 0.847)
 No Information Rate : 0.114
 P-Value [Acc > NIR] : <2e-16

               Kappa : 0.818
 Mcnemar's Test P-Value : NA
```

Statistics by Class:

	Class: 0	Class: 1	Class: 2	Class: 3	Class: 4
Sensitivity	0.9555	0.904	0.8041	0.8031	0.8235
Specificity	0.9851	0.995	0.9837	0.9748	0.9783
Pos Pred Value	0.8632	0.959	0.8540	0.7864	0.8000
Neg Pred Value	0.9956	0.988	0.9769	0.9772	0.9814
Prevalence	0.0898	0.114	0.1062	0.1036	0.0952
Detection Rate	0.0858	0.103	0.0854	0.0832	0.0784
Detection Prevalence	0.0994	0.107	0.1000	0.1058	0.0980
Balanced Accuracy	0.9703	0.949	0.8939	0.8889	0.9009

	Class: 5	Class: 6	Class: 7	Class: 8	Class: 9
Sensitivity	0.7579	0.8812	0.8612	0.7436	0.8167
Specificity	0.9776	0.9940	0.9834	0.9724	0.9743
Pos Pred Value	0.7666	0.9446	0.8612	0.7357	0.7756
Neg Pred Value	0.9766	0.9863	0.9834	0.9735	0.9799
Prevalence	0.0884	0.1044	0.1066	0.0936	0.0982
Detection Rate	0.0670	0.0920	0.0918	0.0696	0.0802
Detection Prevalence	0.0874	0.0974	0.1066	0.0946	0.1034
Balanced Accuracy	0.8678	0.9376	0.9223	0.8580	0.8955

Since we fitted several models earlier of varying complexity, we could examine the degree of overfitting or overly optimistic accuracy from in-sample versus out-of-sample performance measures across them. The code is not shown as it is just a repetition of what we have already done, but it is available in the code bundle provided with the book. The results are shown in *Figure 2.6*:

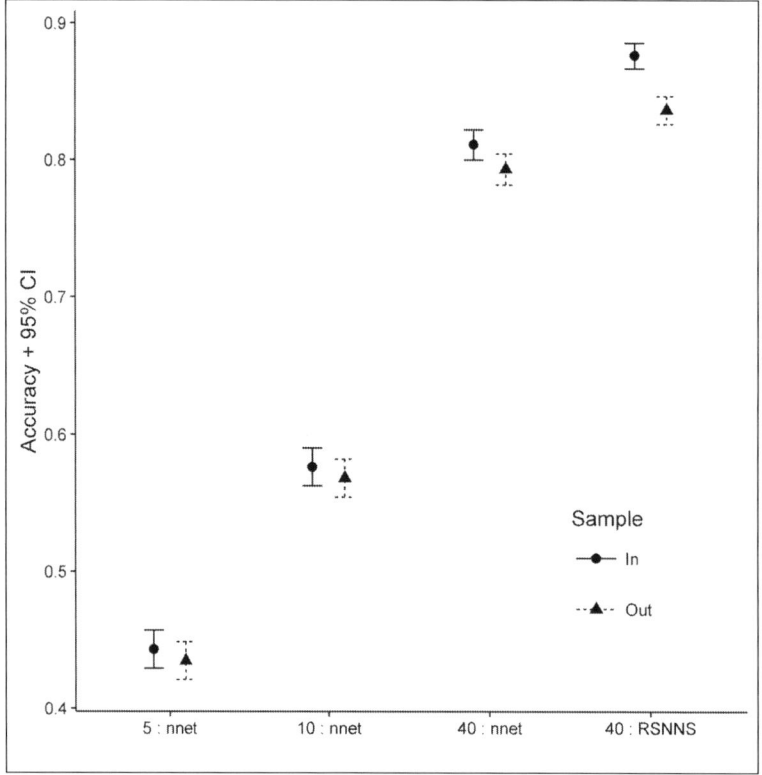

Figure 2.6

Use case – build and apply a neural network

To close out the chapter, we will discuss a more realistic use case for neural networks. We will use a public dataset by *Anguita, D., Ghio, A., Oneto, L., Parra, X., and Reyes-Ortiz, J. L.* (2013) that uses smartphones to track physical activity. The data can be downloaded here: `http://archive.ics.uci.edu/ml/datasets/Human+Activity+Recognition+Using+Smartphones`. The smartphones had an accelerometer and gyroscope from which 561 features from both time and frequency were used.

The smartphones were worn during walking, walking upstairs, walking downstairs, standing, sitting, and lying down. Although this data came from phones, similar measures could be derived from other devices designed to track activity such as various fitness tracking watches or bands. So this data can be useful if we want to sell devices and have them automatically track how many of these different activities the wearer engages in.

This data has been normalized to range from -1 to +1; however, usually we might want to perform some normalization. After downloading the data, the files can be unzipped and we can then locate them in the working directory or modify the paths in the following code to point to the correct location. We can read in the training and testing data, as well as the labels, and to recap take a quick look at the distribution of the outcome (*Figure 2.7*):

```
use.train.x <- read.table("UCI HAR Dataset/train/X_train.txt")
use.train.y <- read.table("UCI HAR Dataset/train/y_train.txt")[[1]]

use.test.x <- read.table("UCI HAR Dataset/test/X_test.txt")
use.test.y <- read.table("UCI HAR Dataset/test/y_test.txt")[[1]]

use.labels <- read.table("UCI HAR Dataset/activity_labels.txt")

barplot(table(use.train.y))
```

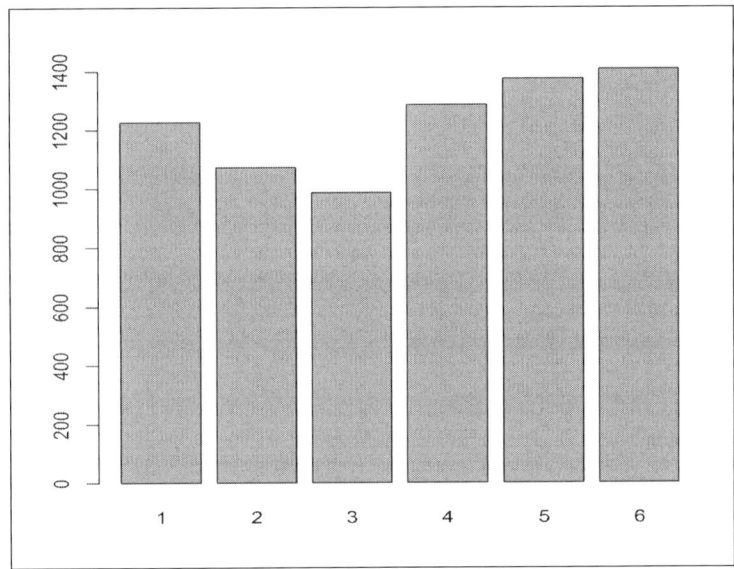

Figure 2.7

We are going to evaluate a variety of tuning parameters to show how we might experiment with different approaches to try to get the best possible model. Because the models can take some time to train and as currently shown only use a single core, we can evaluate the models using different tuning parameters simultaneously using parallel processing. First, we need to add some additional packages to our checkpoint.R file and re-run that:

```
## Chapter 2 ##
library(parallel)
library(foreach)
library(doSNOW)
```

Now we can pick our tuning parameters and set up a local cluster as the backend for the **foreach** R package for parallel for loops. Note that, if you do this on a machine with fewer than five cores, you should change makeCluster(5) to a lower number:

```
## choose tuning parameters
tuning <- list(
  size = c(40, 20, 20, 50, 50),
  maxit = c(60, 100, 100, 100, 100),
  shuffle = c(FALSE, FALSE, TRUE, FALSE, FALSE),
  params = list(FALSE, FALSE, FALSE, FALSE, c(0.1, 20, 3)))


## setup cluster using 5 cores
## load packages, export required data and variables
## and register as a backend for use with the foreach package
cl <- makeCluster(5)
clusterEvalQ(cl, {
  library(RSNNS)
})
clusterExport(cl,
  c("tuning", "use.train.x", "use.train.y",
    "use.test.x", "use.test.y")
  )
registerDoSNOW(cl)
```

Now we are ready to train all the models. The following code shows a parallel for loop, using code that is similar to what we have already seen, but this time setting some of the arguments based on the tuning parameters we previously stored in the list:

```
use.models <- foreach(i = 1:5, .combine = 'c') %dopar% {
  if (tuning$params[[i]][1]) {
    set.seed(1234)
    list(Model = mlp(
      as.matrix(use.train.x),
      decodeClassLabels(use.train.y),
      size = tuning$size[[i]],
      learnFunc = "Rprop",
      shufflePatterns = tuning$shuffle[[i]],
      learnFuncParams = tuning$params[[i]],
      maxit = tuning$maxit[[i]]
      ))
  } else {
    set.seed(1234)
    list(Model = mlp(
      as.matrix(use.train.x),
      decodeClassLabels(use.train.y),
      size = tuning$size[[i]],
      learnFunc = "Rprop",
      shufflePatterns = tuning$shuffle[[i]],
      maxit = tuning$maxit[[i]]
      ))
  }
}
```

Because generating out-of-sample predictions can also take some time, we will do that in parallel as well. However, first we need to export the model results to each of the workers on our cluster, and then we can calculate the predictions:

```
clusterExport(cl, "use.models")
use.yhat <- foreach(i = 1:5, .combine = 'c') %dopar% {
  list(list(
    Insample = encodeClassLabels(fitted.values(use.models[[i]])),
    Outsample = encodeClassLabels(predict(use.models[[i]],
                                          newdata = as.matrix(use.
test.x)))
    ))
}
```

Finally, we can merge the actual and fitted or predicted values together into a dataset, calculate performance measures on each one, and store the overall results together for examination and comparison. We can repeat almost identical code as follows to generate out-of-sample performance measures. That code is not shown in the book, but is available in the code bundle provided with the book. Some additional data management is required here as sometimes a model may not predict each possible response level, but this can make for non-symmetrical frequency cross tabs, unless we convert the variable to a factor and specify the levels. We also drop 0 values, which indicate the model was uncertain how to classify an observation:

```
use.insample <- cbind(Y = use.train.y,
  do.call(cbind.data.frame, lapply(use.yhat, `[[`, "Insample")))
colnames(use.insample) <- c("Y", paste0("Yhat", 1:5))


performance.insample <- do.call(rbind, lapply(1:5, function(i) {
  f <- substitute(~ Y + x, list(x = as.name(paste0("Yhat", i))))
  use.dat <- use.insample[use.insample[,paste0("Yhat", i)] != 0, ]
  use.dat$Y <- factor(use.dat$Y, levels = 1:6)
  use.dat[, paste0("Yhat", i)] <- factor(use.dat[, paste0("Yhat", i)],
levels = 1:6)
  res <- caret::confusionMatrix(xtabs(f, data = use.dat))

  cbind(Size = tuning$size[[i]],
        Maxit = tuning$maxit[[i]],
        Shuffle = tuning$shuffle[[i]],
        as.data.frame(t(res$overall[c("AccuracyNull", "Accuracy",
"AccuracyLower", "AccuracyUpper")]))))
}))
```

If we print the in-sample and out-of-sample performance, we can see how each of our models did and the effect of varying some of the tuning parameters. The output is shown in the following code. The fourth column (null accuracy) is dropped as it is not as important for this comparison. Note that the code for the out-of-sample performance is not shown in this book but is left as an exercise for the reader (an easy adaptation of the code for in-sample performance) and is provided in the code bundle:

```
performance.insample[,-4]


  Size Maxit Shuffle Accuracy AccuracyLower AccuracyUpper
```

1	40	60	FALSE	0.99	0.98	0.99
2	20	100	FALSE	0.99	0.99	0.99
3	20	100	TRUE	0.99	0.99	0.99
4	50	100	FALSE	0.99	0.99	1.00
5	50	100	FALSE	1.00	1.00	1.00

```
performance.outsample[,-4]
```

	Size	Maxit	Shuffle	Accuracy	AccuracyLower	AccuracyUpper
1	**40**	**60**	**FALSE**	**0.93**	**0.92**	**0.94**
2	20	100	FALSE	0.92	0.91	0.93
3	20	100	TRUE	0.92	0.91	0.93
4	50	100	FALSE	0.91	0.90	0.92
5	50	100	FALSE	0.92	0.91	0.93

First of all, these results show that we are able to classify the types of activity people are engaged in quite accurately based on the data from their smartphones. It also seems from the in-sample data that the more complex models do better. However, examining the out-of-sample performance measures, the reverse is actually true! Thus, not only are the in-sample performance measures biased estimates of the models' actual out-of-sample performance, they do not even provide the best way to rank order model performance to choose the best performing model. We will get into ways to combat this overfitting in the next chapter as we prepare to go into deep neural networks where there are multiple hidden layers.

Despite the slightly worse out-of-sample performance, the models still do well—far better than chance alone—and, for our example use case, we could pick the best model (number 1) and be quite confident that using this will provide a good classification of a user's activities.

Summary

This chapter showed how to get started building and training neural networks to classify data including image recognition and physical activity data. One pitfall in machine learning is that more complex models will be more likely to overfit the training data, so that evaluating performance in the same data used to train the model results in biased, overly optimistic estimates of the model performance. Indeed, this can even make a difference as to which model is chosen as the *best*. Overfitting is also an issue for deep neural networks, and in the next chapter we will discuss various techniques used to prevent overfitting—termed regularization—and obtain more accurate estimates of model performance.

3
Preventing Overfitting

In the previous chapter, we learned how to train a basic neural network. We also saw the diminishing returns from further training iterations or a larger neural network in terms of its predictive ability on holdout or validation data not used to train the model. This highlights how, although a more complex model will almost always fit the data it was trained on better, it may not actually predict new data better. This chapter shows different approaches that can be used to prevent models from overfitting the data to improve generalizability, called regularization on unsupervised data. More specifically, whereas models are typically trained by optimizing parameters in a way that reduces the *training* error, regularization is concerned with reducing *testing* or *validation* errors so that the model performs well with new data as well as training data.

The first part of the chapter provides a conceptual overview of a variety of regularization strategies. The chapter closes with an example use case using regularization to improve out-of-sample performance. It covers the following topics:

- L1 penalty
- L2 penalty
- Ensembles and model averaging
- Use case – improving out-of-sample model performance using dropout

L1 penalty

The basic concept of the L1 penalty, also known as the **Least Absolute Shrinkage and Selection Operator** (**lasso**) — (*Hastie, T., Tibshirani, R.,* and *Friedman, J.* (2009)), is that a penalty is used to shrink weights towards zero. The penalty term uses the sum of the absolute weights, so the degree of penalty is no smaller or larger for small or large weights, with the result that small weights may get shrunken to zero, a convenient effect as, in addition to preventing overfitting, it can be a sort of variable selection. The strength of the penalty is controlled by a hyperparameter, λ, which multiplies the sum of the absolute weights, and can be set a priori or, as with other hyperparameters, optimized using cross validation or some similar approach.

Mathematically, it is easier to start with an **Ordinary Least Squares** (**OLS**) regression model. In regression, a set of coefficients or model weights are estimated using the least squared error criteria, where the weight/coefficient vector, B, is estimated such that it minimizes: $(Y - XB)^T(Y - XB)$ where Y is the outcome or dependent variable, X is a $k + 1$ column design matrix with k columns for the predictors and one constant column for the intercept (also called an offset sometimes). The difference between the observed outcome and the predicted values (the product of the design matrix post multiplied by the weight vector) is a vector of the errors or residuals. In this framework, one way to think about the L1 penalty is that it is a constrained estimator, where the weight vector, B, is estimated subject to the constraint that the sum of the absolute weights is less than or equal to some (user-chosen) threshold, λ.

Typically, the intercept or offset term is excluded from this constraint (for example, by pre-centering all data and dropping the intercept or by selectively applying the constraint). Another way of viewing the L1 penalty is to see it as a modification to the function minimized, from $(Y - XB)^T(Y - XB)$ to $(Y - XB)^T(Y - XB) + \lambda ||B||_1$, where $||B||_1$ represents the sum of the absolute weights. If $\lambda = 0$, then the L1 penalty reduces to the regular OLS estimator. The user may choose λ, or more commonly it is treated as a hyperparameter and optimized by evaluating a range of possible λ values (for example, through cross validation). Although outside the scope of this book, the L1 penalty may also be viewed through a Bayesian perspective, the final posterior estimates are a function of the estimates from the data and the prior, and the shrinkage that occurs from the penalty term is accomplished by setting a prior with varying degrees of certainty. Technically, the parameters could be shrunk towards any arbitrary value, but they are almost always shrunk towards zero.

Even if the theory behind why and how the L1 penalty works is not so clear, there are a number of practical implications that are straightforward. First, it may be obvious that the effect of the penalty depends on the size of the weights, and the size of the weights depends on the scale of the data. Therefore, data is typically standardized to have unit variance first (or at least to make the variance of each variable equal). The L1 penalty has a tendency to shrink small weights to zero (for explanations as to why this happens, see *Hastie, T., Tibshirani, R., and Friedman, J. (2009)*). If you only consider variables for which the L1 penalty leaves non zero weights, it can essentially function as feature selection, a primary motivation of another name commonly used for the L1 penalty, the Least Absolute Shrinkage and Selection Operator, or lasso. Even outside the usage of strict feature selection, the tendency for the L1 penalty to shrink small coefficients to zero can be convenient for simplifying the interpretation of the model results.

When considering the L1 penalty as constrained optimization, it is easy to see how it effectively limits the complexity of the model. Even if many predictors are included, the sum of the absolute weights cannot exceed the defined threshold. One result of this is that, using the L1 penalty, it is actually possible to include more predictors than cases or observations, so long as there is a sufficiently strong penalty term; the apparently (by number of weights) over-parameterized model becomes uniquely estimable through the constraints.

With these basics on the L1 penalty, we will now briefly consider how the L1 penalty can apply to neural networks, the main use case we are concerned with in this book. Let X represent our inputs, Y our outcome or dependent variable, and B our parameters, and F, the objective function which will be optimized to obtain B. Specifically: $F(B; X, Y)$. In neural networks, parameters may be biases or offsets (essentially intercepts from regression) and the weights. The L1 penalty modifies the objective function to be: $F(B; X, Y) + \lambda ||w||_1$, where w represents only the weights (that is, typically offsets are ignored). Considering the gradient, we can show that the additional penalty term is $\lambda * sign(w)$. This highlights the fact that the penalty is constant regardless of the magnitude of the weight. This will be an important point of distinction compared with the L2 penalty, which we will discuss next. Further, it is part of the way in which the L1 penalty tends to result in a sparse solution (that is, more zero weights) as small and larger weights result in equal penalties, so that at each update of the gradient the weights are moved towards zero.

We have discussed λ as a constant, controlling the degree of penalty or regularization. However, it is possible to set different values. Although not commonly done in a single layer neural network (it is atypical to seek to differentially regularize specific weights), it becomes more useful with deep neural networks, where varying degrees of regularization can be applied to different layers. One reason for considering such differential regularization is that it is sometimes desirable to allow a greater number of parameters (say by including more neurons in a particular layer) but then counteract this somewhat through stronger regularization. Despite this, as these hyperparameters are typically optimized through cross validation or other empirical techniques, it can be quite computationally demanding to allow them to vary for every layer of a deep neural network, as the number of possible values grows exponentially; so most commonly a single value is used across the entire model. After exploring the L1 penalty practically in R, we move on to consider another common form of regularization, the L2 penalty.

L1 penalty in action

To see how the L1 penalty works, we can use a simulated linear regression problem. First, we will add the R package **glmnet** to the checkpoint.R file to load the relevant library and use a reproducible version, as before:

```
library(glmnet)
```

Next we can simulate the data, using a purposefully pathologically correlated set of predictors:

```
set.seed(1234)

X <- mvrnorm(n = 200, mu = c(0, 0, 0, 0, 0),
  Sigma = matrix(c(
    1, .9999, .99, .99, .10,
    .9999, 1, .99, .99, .10,
    .99, .99, 1, .99, .10,
    .99, .99, .99, 1, .10,
    .10, .10, .10, .10, 1
  ), ncol = 5))

y <- rnorm(200, 3 + X %*% matrix(c(1, 1, 1, 1, 0)), .5)
```

Next, we can fit an OLS regression model to the first 100 cases, and then use the lasso. To use the lasso, we use the `glmnet()` function from the glmnet package. This function can actually fit the L1 or the L2 (discussed in the next section) penalties, and which occurs is determined by the argument, `alpha`. When `alpha = 1`, it is the L1 penalty (that is, the lasso), and when `alpha = 0` it is the L2 penalty (that is, ridge regression). Further, because we do not know the value of lambda we should pick, we can evaluate a range of options and tune this hyperparameter automatically using cross validation, accomplished by using the `cv.glmnet()` function:

```
m.ols <- lm(y[1:100] ~ X[1:100, ])
```

```
m.lasso.cv <- cv.glmnet(X[1:100, ], y[1:100], alpha = 1)
```

We can plot the lasso object to see the mean squared error for a variety of lambda values:

```
plot(m.lasso.cv)
```

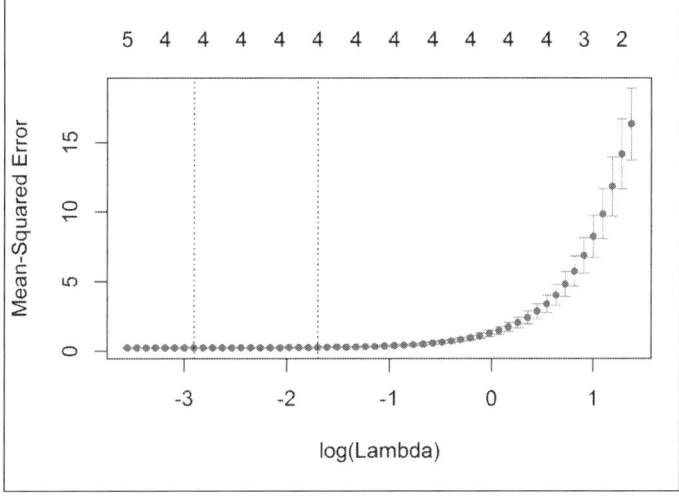

Figure 3.1

One thing that we can see from the graph is that, when the penalty gets too high, the cross-validated model error increases. Indeed, the lasso seems to do well with very low lambda values, perhaps indicating the lasso does not help improve out-of-sample performance/generalizability much. For the sake of this example, we will continue but in actual use this might give us pause to consider whether the lasso was really helping.

Finally, we can compare the OLS coefficients with those from the lasso:

```
cbind(
  OLS = coef(m.ols),
  Lasso = coef(m.lasso.cv)[,1])
```

```
                OLS  Lasso
(Intercept)   2.958   2.99
X[1:100, ]1  -0.082   1.41
X[1:100, ]2   2.239   0.71
X[1:100, ]3   0.602   0.51
X[1:100, ]4   1.235   1.17
X[1:100, ]5  -0.041   0.00
```

Notice that the OLS coefficients are noisier and also that, in the lasso, predictor 5 is penalized to 0. Recall from the simulated data that the *true* coefficients are 3, 1, 1, 1, 1, and 0. The OLS estimates have much too low a value for the first predictor and much too high a value for the second, whereas the lasso has more accurate values for each.

L2 penalty

The L2 penalty, also known as ridge regression, is similar in many ways to the L1 penalty, but instead of adding a penalty based on the sum of the absolute weights, the penalty is based on the squared weights. This has the effect of providing a varied penalty, with larger (positive or negative) weights resulting in a greater penalty. In the context of neural networks, this is sometimes referred to as weight decay. If you examine the gradient of the regularized objective function, there is a penalty such that, at every update, there is a multiplicative penalty to the weights. As for the L1 penalty, although they could be included, biases or offsets are usually excluded from this.

From the perspective of a linear regression problem, the L2 penalty is a modification to the objective function minimized, from $(Y - XB)^T(Y - XB)$ to $(Y - XB)^T(Y - XB) + 0.5\lambda B^T B$. As with the L1 penalty, the L2 penalty can allow otherwise undetermined problems to be solved, particularly when the covariance matrix of the predictors is singular. The reason for this is that the effect of the L2 penalty is essentially to increase the variance of each variable. In OLS, the normal equations for B in matrix form are $inv(X^TX)X^Ty$ but solving the regularized OLS objective function shown earlier, obtain, $inv(X^TX + \lambda I)X^Ty$, where I is the identity matrix.

Since X^TX is the variance-covariance matrix for the design matrix, adding λI will have the effect of increasing the diagonal, but leaving the off diagonals unchanged. That is, the variances are increased but covariances unchanged, resulting in shrinking the correlations (standardized covariances) towards zero. A sufficiently strong penalty will result in otherwise singular covariance matrices being uniquely estimable, and can also help stabilize estimates when there are strongly correlated predictors.

L2 penalty in action

To see how the L2 penalty works, we can use the same simulated linear regression problem we used for the L1 penalty. To fit a ridge regression model, we use the `glmnet()` function from the glmnet package. As mentioned previously, this function can actually fit the L1 or the L2 penalties, and which occurs is determined by the argument, `alpha`. When `alpha = 1`, it fits the lasso, and when `alpha = 0`, it fits ridge regression. This time, we choose `alpha = 0`. Again, we evaluate a range of lambda options and tune this hyperparameter automatically using cross validation, accomplished by using the `cv.glmnet()` function:

```
m.ridge.cv <- cv.glmnet(X[1:100, ], y[1:100], alpha = 0)
```

We plot the ridge regression object to see the error for a variety of lambda values:

```
plot(m.ridge.cv)
```

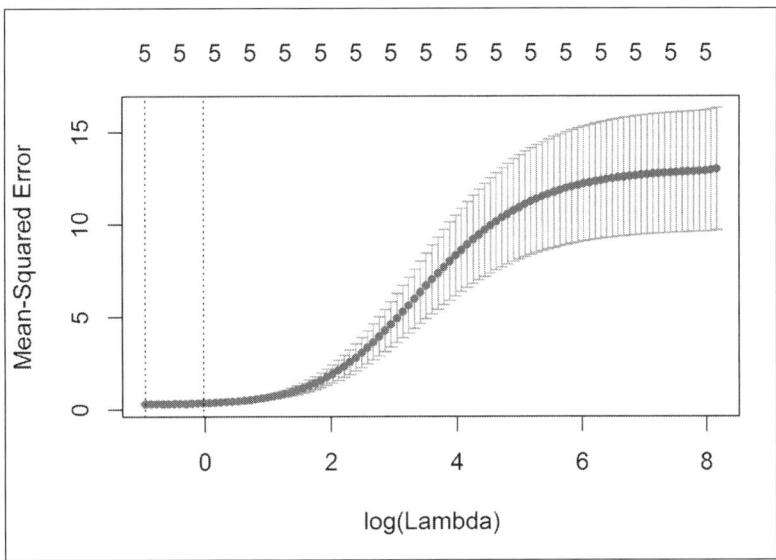

Figure 3.2

Although the shape is different from the lasso in that the error appears to asymptote for higher lambda values, it is still clear that, when the penalty gets too high, the cross-validated model error increases. As with the lasso, the ridge regression model seems to do well with very low lambda values, perhaps indicating the L2 penalty does not much help improve out-of-sample performance/generalizability.

Finally, we can compare the OLS coefficients with those from the lasso and the ridge regression model:

```
cbind(
  OLS = coef(m.ols),
  Lasso = coef(m.lasso.cv)[,1],
  Ridge = coef(m.ridge.cv)[,1])
```

```
                OLS Lasso Ridge
(Intercept)   2.958  2.99 3.002
X[1:100, ]1  -0.082  1.41 0.958
X[1:100, ]2   2.239  0.71 0.964
X[1:100, ]3   0.602  0.51 0.924
X[1:100, ]4   1.235  1.17 0.949
X[1:100, ]5  -0.041  0.00 0.011
```

Although ridge regression does not shrink the coefficient for the fifth predictor to exactly zero, it is smaller than in the OLS, and the remaining parameters are all slightly shrunken, but quite close to their true values of 3, 1, 1, 1, and 0.

Weight decay (L2 penalty in neural networks)

Without knowing it, we have actually already seen regularization in action in *Chapter 2, Training a Prediction Model*. The neural network we trained using the caret and nnet package used a weight decay of 0.10. We can investigate the use of the weight decay by varying it, and tuning it using cross-validation. First we load the data as before. Then we create a local cluster to run the cross validation in parallel. Note that, as before, rather than load the libraries directly, we need to `source()` the `checkpoint.R` file so that each of the workers in our cluster is using the same R package version:

```
## same data as from previous chapter
digits.train <- read.csv("train.csv")
```

```
## convert to factor
digits.train$label <- factor(digits.train$label, levels = 0:9)


i <- 1:5000
digits.X <- digits.train[i, -1]
digits.y <- digits.train[i, 1]


## try various weight decays and number of iterations
## register backend so that different decays can be
## estimated in parallel
cl <- makeCluster(4)
clusterEvalQ(cl, {
  source("checkpoint.R")
})
registerDoSNOW(cl)
```

Next we train a neural network on the digit classification, and vary the weight decay penalty at 0 (no penalty) and 0.10. We also loop through two sets of the number of iterations allowed: 100 or 150. Note that this code is computationally intensive and depending on hardware may take some time to run:

```
set.seed(1234)
digits.decay.m1 <- lapply(c(100, 150), function(its) {
  train(digits.X, digits.y,
          method = "nnet",
          tuneGrid = expand.grid(
            .size = c(10),
            .decay = c(0, .1)),
          trControl = trainControl(method = "cv", number = 5, repeats =
1),
          MaxNWts = 10000,
          maxit = its)
})
```

Examining the results, we see that, when we limit to only 100 iterations, the non-regularized model (Accuracy = 0.63) outperforms the regularized model (Accuracy = 0.60) based on cross-validated results (although neither is doing well absolutely, particularly on this data):

```
digits.decay.m1[[1]]
Neural Network


5000 samples
 784 predictor
  10 classes: '0', '1', '2', '3', '4', '5', '6', '7', '8', '9'


No pre-processing
Resampling: Cross-Validated (5 fold)
Summary of sample sizes: 4000, 3999, 4000, 4001, 4000
Resampling results across tuning parameters:


  decay  Accuracy  Kappa  Accuracy SD  Kappa SD
  0.0    0.63      0.59   0.052        0.058
  0.1    0.60      0.56   0.061        0.068


Tuning parameter 'size' was held constant at a value of 10
Accuracy was used to select the optimal model using  the
 largest value.
The final values used for the model were size = 10 and decay = 0.
```

Next we can examine the model with 150 iterations and see whether the regularized or non-regularized model performs better:

```
digits.decay.m1[[2]]
Neural Network


5000 samples
 784 predictor
  10 classes: '0', '1', '2', '3', '4', '5', '6', '7', '8', '9'
```

```
No pre-processing
Resampling: Cross-Validated (5 fold)
Summary of sample sizes: 4002, 4000, 4000, 3999, 3999
Resampling results across tuning parameters:
```

decay	Accuracy	Kappa	Accuracy SD	Kappa SD
0.0	0.65	0.61	0.049	0.055
0.1	0.66	0.62	0.071	0.078

```
Tuning parameter 'size' was held constant at a value of 10
Accuracy was used to select the optimal model using  the
 largest value.
The final values used for the model were size = 10 and decay = 0.1.
```

Overall, the model with more iterations outperforms the model with fewer iterations, regardless of the regularization. However, comparing both models with 150 iterations, the regularized model is superior (Accuracy = 0.66) to the non-regularized model (Accuracy = 0.65), although here the difference is relatively small.

These results highlight the point that regularization is often most helpful with more complex models that have greater flexibility to fit (and overfit) the data, and that (in models that are appropriate or overly simplistic for the data) regularization may actually decrease performance. In the next section, we will discuss ensemble and model averaging techniques, the last forms of regularization we will highlight in this book.

Ensembles and model averaging

Another approach to regularization involves creating ensembles of models and combining them, such as by model averaging or some other algorithm for combining individual model results. As with many of the previous regularization methods, model averaging is a fairly simple concept. If you have different models that each generate a set of predictions, each model may make errors in its predictions, but they might not all make the same errors. Where one model predicts too high a value, another may predict one that's too low, so that, if averaged, some of the errors cancel out resulting in a more accurate prediction than would have been otherwise obtained.

To better understand model averaging, let's consider a couple of different but extreme examples. In the first case, suppose that the models being averaged are identical or at least generate identical predictions (that is, perfectly correlated). In that case, the average will result in no benefit, but also no harm. In the second case, suppose that the models being averaged each independently perform equally well, and their predictions are uncorrelated (or have very low correlations). Then the average will be far more accurate as it gains the strengths of each model. The following code gives an example using simulated data. In this small example, we only have three models, but they illustrate the point:

```
## simulated data
set.seed(1234)
d <- data.frame(
  x = rnorm(400))
d$y <- with(d, rnorm(400, 2 + ifelse(x < 0, x + x^2, x + x^2.5), 1))
d.train <- d[1:200, ]
d.test <- d[201:400, ]


## three different models
m1 <- lm(y ~ x, data = d.train)
m2 <- lm(y ~ I(x^2), data = d.train)
m3 <- lm(y ~ pmax(x, 0) + pmin(x, 0), data = d.train)


## In sample R2
cbind(
  M1 = summary(m1)$r.squared,
  M2 = summary(m2)$r.squared,
  M3 = summary(m3)$r.squared)


       M1   M2   M3
[1,] 0.33 0.60 0.76
```

We can see that the predictive value of each model, at least in the training data, varies quite a bit. Evaluating the correlations among fitted values in the training data can also help to indicate how much overlap there is among the model predictions:

```
## correlations in the training data
cor(cbind(
```

```
  M1 = fitted(m1),
  M2 = fitted(m2),
  M3 = fitted(m3)))


     M1   M2   M3
M1 1.00 0.11 0.65
M2 0.11 1.00 0.78
M3 0.65 0.78 1.00
```

Next we generate predicted values for the testing data, the average of the predicted values, and again correlate the predictions along with reality in the testing data:

```
## generate predictions and the average prediction
d.test$yhat1 <- predict(m1, newdata = d.test)
d.test$yhat2 <- predict(m2, newdata = d.test)
d.test$yhat3 <- predict(m3, newdata = d.test)
d.test$yhatavg <- rowMeans(d.test[, paste0("yhat", 1:3)])

## correlation in the testing data
cor(d.test)
```

	x	y	yhat1	yhat2	yhat3	yhatavg
x	1.000	0.44	1.000	-0.098	0.60	0.55
y	0.442	1.00	0.442	0.753	0.87	0.91
yhat1	1.000	0.44	1.000	-0.098	0.60	0.55
yhat2	-0.098	0.75	-0.098	1.000	0.69	0.76
yhat3	0.596	0.87	0.596	0.687	1.00	0.98
yhatavg	0.552	0.91	0.552	0.765	0.98	1.00

From the results we can see that indeed the average of the three models' predictions performs better than any of the models individually. However, this is only guaranteed to be true when each model performs similarly well. For example, consider a pathological case where one model predicts the outcome perfectly and another is random noise that is completely uncorrelated with the outcome. In this case, averaging the two would certainly result in worse performance than just using the good model. In general, it is good to check that the models being averaged have similar performance, at least in the training data. The second lesson is that, given models with similar performance, it is desirable to have lower correlations between model predictions, as this will result in the best performing average.

Ensemble methods are methods that employ model averaging. One common technique is known as bootstrap aggregating, where the data is sampled with replacement to form equally sized datasets, a model is trained on each, and then these results are averaged. Because the data is sampled with replacement, some cases may show up multiple times or not at all in each dataset. Because a model is trained on each dataset, if a particular variation is unique to just a few cases or a rare *quirk* of the data, it may only emerge in one model; when the predictions are averaged across many models trained on each of the resampled datasets, such overfitting will tend to be reduced. This process is known as **bagging** (bootstrap aggregating). In some contexts (for example, decision trees), further steps may be taken to attempt to reduce the correlations among the different models. For example, random forests are decision trees that use bootstrap aggregating but also randomly select a subset of features at each node split in order to try to reduce model to model correlations and thus improve the overall average performance.

Bagging and model averaging is not used as frequently in deep neural networks because the computational cost of training each model can be quite high and thus repeating the process many times becomes prohibitively expensive in terms of time and compute resources. However, the dropout process discussed in the next section serves a very similar function to the way many subset models are trained, by dropping specific neurons, and then the results of these models are averaged. Nevertheless, it is still possible to use model averaging in the context of deep neural networks, even if perhaps it is on only a handful of models rather than hundreds, as is common in random forests and some other approaches.

Use case – improving out-of-sample model performance using dropout

Dropout is a relatively novel approach to regularization that is particularly valuable for large and complex deep neural networks. For a much more detailed exploration of dropout in deep neural networks, see *Srivastava, N., Hinton, G., Krizhevsky, A., Sutskever, I.,* and *Salakhutdinov, R.* (2014). The concept behind dropout is actually quite straightforward. During the training of the model, units (for example, inputs, hidden neurons, and so on) are probabilistically dropped along with all connections to and from them. For example, *Figure 3.3* is an example of what might happen at each step of training for a model where hidden neurons and their connections are probabilistically dropped with a probability of 1/3. The grayed out and dashed neurons and connections are the ones that were dropped. Importantly, it is not that some neurons are dropped during the entirety of training, but that they are only dropped for a step/update:

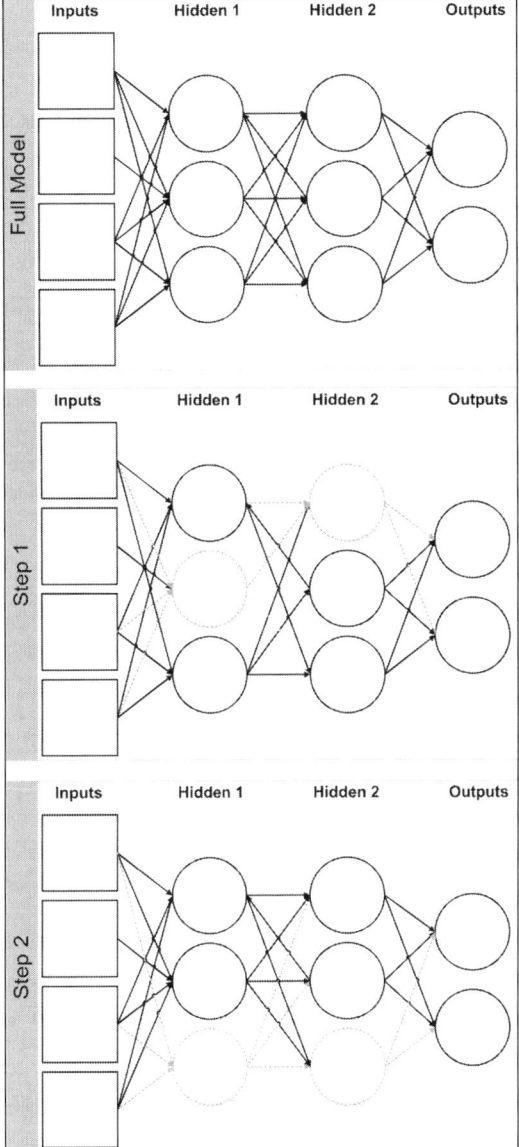

Figure 3.3

One way to think about dropout is that it forces models to be more robust to perturbations. Although many neurons are included in the full model, during training they are not all simultaneously present, and so neurons must operate somewhat more independently than they would have to otherwise. It is also worth noting that inputs can be dropped as well as hidden neurons, but typically this is either not done or done to a much lesser extent.

Another way of viewing dropout is that, if you have a large model with *N* weights between hidden neurons, but 50% are dropped during training, although all *N* weights will be used during some stages of training, you have effectively halved the total model complexity as the average number of weights will be halved. This reduces model complexity, and hence may help to prevent overfitting of the data. Because of this feature, if the proportion of dropout is *p*, *Srivastava, N., Hinton, G., Krizhevsky, A., Sutskever, I.*, and *Salakhutdinov, R.* (2014) recommend scaling up the target model complexity by *1/p* in order to end up with a roughly equally complex model.

Although neurons can be randomly dropped during training, during testing it is computationally inconvenient to calculate many predictions based on models dropping some neurons and then average the predictions from each model. Instead, it has been suggested (and this seems to perform well) that we should use an approximate average based on scaling the weights from a single neural network based on each weight's probability of being included (that is, *1 – p*, although this can be done empirically rather than theoretically).

In addition to working well, this approximate weight re-scaling is a fairly trivial calculation. Thus, the primary computational cost of dropout comes from the fact that a model with more neurons and weights must be used because so many (a commonly recommended value is around 50% for hidden neurons) are dropped during each training update.

Although dropout is fairly computationally cheap, it can be slower as, because of the dropout, a larger model may be required, and larger models typically are slower or more computationally demanding to train. To counteract this, a higher learning rate can be used so that fewer iterations are required. One potential downside of such an approach is that, with fewer neurons and a faster learning rate, some weights may become quite large. Fortunately, it is possible to use dropout along with other forms of regularization, such as the L1 or L2 penalty. Taken together, the result is a larger model that that can quickly (a faster learning rate) explore a broader parameter space, but is regularized through dropout and a penalty to keep the weights in check.

To show the use of dropout in a neural network, we will return to the **Modified National Institute of Standards and Technology (MNIST)** dataset (that we downloaded in *Chapter 2, Training a Prediction Model*, from Kaggle) we worked with previously. We will use the `nn.train()` function from the deepnet package, as it allows for dropout. As in the previous chapter, we will run the four models in parallel to reduce the time it takes. Specifically, we compare four models, two with and two without dropout regularization and with either 40 or 80 hidden neurons. For dropout, we specify the proportion to dropout separately for the hidden and visible units. Based on the rule of thumb that about 50% of hidden units (and 80% of observed units) should be kept, we specify the dropout proportions at `.5` and `.2`, respectively:

```
## Fit Models
nn.models <- foreach(i = 1:4, .combine = 'c') %dopar% {
set.seed(1234)
 list(nn.train(
    x = as.matrix(digits.X),
    y = model.matrix(~ 0 + digits.y),
    hidden = c(40, 80, 40, 80)[i],
    activationfun = "tanh",
    learningrate = 0.8,
    momentum = 0.5,
    numepochs = 150,
    output = "softmax",
    hidden_dropout = c(0, 0, .5, .5)[i],
    visible_dropout = c(0, 0, .2, .2)[i]))
}
```

Next, we can loop through the models and obtain predicted values and get the overall model performance:

```
nn.yhat <- lapply(nn.models, function(obj) {
  encodeClassLabels(nn.predict(obj, as.matrix(digits.X)))
})


perf.train <- do.call(cbind, lapply(nn.yhat, function(yhat) {
  caret::confusionMatrix(xtabs(~ I(yhat - 1) + digits.y))$overall
}))
colnames(perf.train) <- c("N40", "N80", "N40_Reg", "N80_Reg")


options(digits = 4)
perf.train
```

	N40	N80	N40_Reg	N80_Reg
Accuracy	0.9050	0.9546	0.9212	0.9396
Kappa	0.8944	0.9495	0.9124	0.9329
AccuracyLower	0.8965	0.9485	0.9134	0.9326

```
AccuracyUpper  0.9130 0.9602  0.9285  0.9460

AccuracyNull   0.1116 0.1116  0.1116  0.1116

AccuracyPValue 0.0000 0.0000  0.0000  0.0000

McnemarPValue     NaN    NaN     NaN     NaN
```

When evaluating the models in the in-sample training data, it seems that the 40-neuron model performs better with regularization than without it, but that the 80-neuron model performs better without regularization than with regularization. Of course the real test comes on the testing or hold out data:

```
i2 <- 5001:10000

test.X <- digits.train[i2, -1]

test.y <- digits.train[i2, 1]


nn.yhat.test <- lapply(nn.models, function(obj) {
  encodeClassLabels(nn.predict(obj, as.matrix(test.X)))
})


perf.test <- do.call(cbind, lapply(nn.yhat.test, function(yhat) {
  caret::confusionMatrix(xtabs(~ I(yhat - 1) + test.y))$overall
}))
colnames(perf.test) <- c("N40", "N80", "N40_Reg", "N80_Reg")


perf.test
```

	N40	N80	N40_Reg	N80_Reg
Accuracy	0.8652	0.8684	0.8868	0.9014
Kappa	0.8502	0.8537	0.8742	0.8904
AccuracyLower	0.8554	0.8587	0.8777	0.8928
AccuracyUpper	0.8746	0.8777	0.8955	0.9095
AccuracyNull	0.1074	0.1074	0.1074	0.1074
AccuracyPValue	0.0000	0.0000	0.0000	0.0000
McnemarPValue	NaN	NaN	NaN	NaN

The testing data highlights quite well the fact that, in the non-regularized model, the additional neurons do not meaningfully improve the performance of the model on the testing data. In addition, the in-sample performance was overly optimistic (Accuracy = 0.9546 versus Accuracy = 0.8684 for the 80-neuron, non-regularized model in training and testing data, respectively). However, here we see the advantage of the regularized models for both the 40- and the 80-neuron models. Although both still perform worse in the testing data than they did in the training data, they perform better than the equivalent non-regularized models in the testing data. This difference is particularly important for the 80-neuron model as there is a 0.0862 drop in overall accuracy from training to testing data, but in the regularized model the drop is only 0.0382, resulting in the regularized 80-neuron model having the best overall performance.

Although these numbers are by no means record-setting, they do show the value of using dropout, or regularization more generally, and how one might go about trying to tune the model and dropout parameters to improve the ultimate testing performance.

Summary

This chapter showed several approaches to preventing overfitting including common penalties, the L1 penalty and L2 penalty, ensembles of simpler models, and dropout where variables and/or cases are dropped to make the model noisy and prevent overfitting. We examined the role of penalties in regression problems and for neural networks. In the next chapter, we will move into deep learning and deep neural networks and see how to push the accuracy and performance of our predictive models even further.

4
Identifying Anomalous Data

In this chapter we will delve into deep neural networks and deep learning models. This chapter will focus on auto-encoder models, which can be used to learn the features of a dataset. The first part of the chapter introduces unsupervised learning where there is no specific outcome to be predicted. The next section provides a conceptual overview of auto-encoder models in a machine learning and deep neural network context in particular. The main core of the chapter will show how to build and apply an auto-encoder model to identify anomalous data. Such atypical data may simply be bad data or outliers, but these techniques are also used for fraud detection; for example, when an individual's credit card spending pattern differs from their usual behavior, it may be a red flag that something is wrong. Finally, the chapter closes with some exploration of how to fine-tune the models, including the use of different regularization strategies discussed in the previous chapter. In addition to being useful in its own right, this chapter will provide important building blocks for using and training deep learning models.

This chapter will cover the following topics:

- What is unsupervised learning?
- How do auto-encoders work?
- Training an auto-encoder in R
- Use case – building and applying an auto-encoder model
- Fine-tuning auto-encoder models

Getting started with unsupervised learning

So far we have focused on models and techniques that broadly fall under the category of **supervised learning**. Supervised learning is *supervised* in the sense that the task is for the machine to learn the relationship between a set of variables or features and one or more outcomes. Often, there is only a single outcome. For example, a company may wish to predict whether someone is likely to become a customer, in which case the outcome of whether an individual becomes a customer coded as yes/no. In this chapter, we will delve into methods of **unsupervised learning**. In contrast with supervised learning, where there is an outcome variable(s) or labeled data is used, unsupervised learning does not require any outcomes or labeled data. Unsupervised learning uses only input features for learning. A common example of unsupervised learning is cluster analysis, such as **K-means clustering**, where the machine learns hidden or latent clusters in the data to minimize a criterion (for example, the smallest variance within a cluster).

Another way to think about unsupervised learning is that the goal is to predict the inputs. An example of this is shown in *Figure 4.1*. At first this is counter-intuitive as it may seem relatively unhelpful to learn a sophisticated model whose only purpose is to reproduce the inputs fed into it. However, there are a number of useful features. One common use of unsupervised learning is dimension reduction. The goal of dimension reduction is for a set of p variables to find a set of latent variables, k, so that $k < p$, but with the k latent variables the p raw variables can be reasonably reproduced. This is always a trade-off and balancing act, as typically the greater the dimension reduction, the greater the simplicity, but at the cost of accuracy:

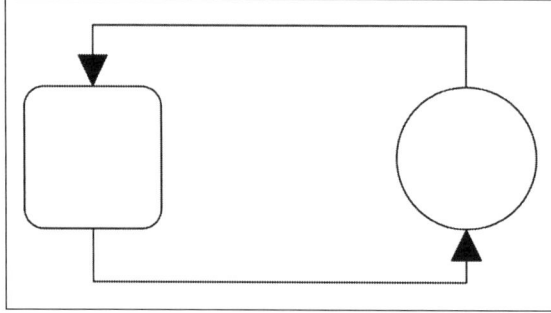

Figure 4.1

Perhaps the most common example of dimension reduction is principal component analysis. Principal component analysis uses an orthogonal transformation to go from the raw data to the principal components. In addition to being uncorrelated, the principal components are ordered from the component that explains the most variance to that which explains the least. Although all principal components can be used (in which case the dimensionality of the data is not reduced), only components that explain a sufficiently large amount of variance (for example, based on high eigenvalues) are included and components that account for relatively little variance are dropped as noise or unnecessary.

A variety of other methods for unsupervised learning are covered in Chapter 14 of *Hastie, T., Tibshirani, R.,* and *Friedman, J.* (2009). The remainder of this chapter will focus on unsupervised methods for deep learning, specifically on auto-encoders.

How do auto-encoders work?

Auto-encoders are neural networks and may be shallow or deep, as with other neural networks we have discussed so far. What distinguishes auto-encoders from other forms of neural network is that auto-encoders are trained to reproduce or predict the inputs. Thus the hidden layers and neurons are not maps between an input and some other outcome, but are self (auto)-encoding.

Unlike the more common cases of neural networks where the outcome is some variable we are interested in predicting; given sufficient complexity, auto-encoders can simply learn the identity function and the hidden neurons will exactly mirror the raw data, resulting in no meaningful benefit. Because the outcome used for training is the same as the inputs, the *best* auto-encoder is not necessarily the most accurate one, but one that reveals some meaningful structure or architecture in the data or one that reduces noise, identifies outliers or anomalous data, or some other useful side effect that is not necessarily directly related to accurate predictions of the model inputs.

One way to use auto-encoders is to perform dimension reduction. Auto-encoders with a lower dimensionality than the raw data are called **undercomplete**; by using an undercomplete auto-encoder, one can force the auto-encoder to learn the most salient or prominent features of the data. These new hidden features can then be used for further analysis or work. For example, an important and common application of auto-encoders is to pre-train deep neural networks or other supervised learning models. In addition, it may be possible and of interest to directly interpret the hidden features themselves; for example, they may provide insight into the key characteristics or structures in the data.

Using an undercomplete model is effectively a way to regularize the model. However, it is also possible to train **overcomplete** auto-encoders where the hidden dimensionality is greater than the raw data, so long as some other form of regularization is used. We will discuss different forms of regularization in more depth in the next section.

As with regular neural networks, there are broadly two parts to auto-encoders. First, an encoding function, $f(\cdot)$, encodes the raw data, x, to the hidden neurons, H. Second, a decoding function, $g(\cdot)$, decodes H back to x.

Regularized auto-encoders

An undercomplete auto-encoder is, in a way, a form of regularized auto-encoder, where the regularization occurs through using a shallower (or in some other way lower) dimensional representation than the data. However, regularization can be accomplished through other means as well.

Penalized auto-encoders

As we have seen in *Chapter 3, Preventing Overfitting*, one approach is to use penalties. In general, our goal is to (as simply as possible) minimize the re-construction error. If we have an objective function, F, traditionally, we may optimize $F(y, f(x))$, where $f(\cdot)$ encodes the raw data inputs to generate predicted or expected y values. For auto-encoders, we have $F(x, g(f(x)))$, so that the machine learns the weights and functional form of $f(\cdot)$ and $g(\cdot)$ to minimize the discrepancy between x and the reconstruction of x, namely $g(f(x))$. If we want to use an overcomplete auto-encoder, we need to introduce some form of regularization to force the machine to learn a representation that does not simply exactly mirror the input. For example, we might add a function that penalizes based on complexity, so that, instead of optimizing $F(x, g(f(x)))$, we optimize $F(x, g(f(x))) + P(f(x))$, where the penalty function, P, depends on the encoding or the raw inputs, $f(\cdot)$. Such penalties differ somewhat from those we have seen before, however, in that the penalty is designed to induce sparseness not of the parameters but rather of the latent variables, H, which are the encoded representations of the raw data. The goal is to learn a latent representation that captures the essential features of the data.

Another type of penalty that can be used to provide regularization is one based on the derivative. Whereas sparse auto-encoders have a penalty that induces sparseness of the latent variables, penalizing the derivatives results in the model learning a form of $f(\cdot)$ that is relatively insensitive to minor perturbations of the raw input data, x, or rather it forces a penalty on functions where the encoding varies greatly for changes in x, preferring regions where the gradient is relatively flat.

Denoising auto-encoders

Denoising auto-encoders remove noise or denoise data, and are a useful technique for learning a latent representation of raw data (*Vincent, P., Larochelle, H., Bengio, Y., and Manzagol, P. A. (2008, July); Bengio, Y., Courville, A., and Vincent, P. (2013)*). We said the general task of an auto-encoder was to optimize: $F(x, g(f(x)))$. However, for a denoising auto-encoder, the task is to recover x from a noisy or corrupted version of x, denoted as $\tilde{x}$. So the task becomes optimizing $F(x, g(f(\tilde{x})))$.

Although denoising auto-encoders are used to try to recover the *true* representation from corrupted data or data with noise, this technique can also be used as a regularization tool. As a method of regularization, rather than having noisy or corrupted data and attempting to recover the truth, the raw data is purposefully corrupted. This forces the auto-encoder to do more than merely learn the identity function, as the raw inputs ($\tilde{x}$) are no longer identical to the output (x). The process is shown in *Figure 4.2*:

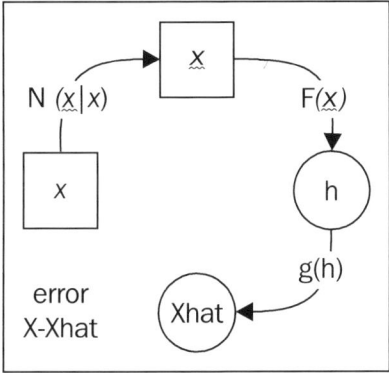

Figure 4.2

The remaining choice is what the function, $N(\cdot)$, which adds the noise or corrupts x, should be. Two choices are to add noise through a stochastic process or for any given training iteration to only include a subset of the raw x inputs. In the next section, we will explore how to actually train auto-encoder models in R.

Training an auto-encoder in R

To train our first auto-encoder, we first need to get R set up. In addition to the other packages in our `checkpoint.R` file, we will add the **data.table** package to facilitate data management, as shown in the following code:

```
library(data.table)
```

Now we can source the `checkpoint.R` file to set up the R environment for analysis, as follows:

```
source("checkpoint.R")
options(width = 70, digits = 2)
```

For these first examples, we will use the **Modified National Institute of Standards and Technology (MNIST)** digits image data. The following code loads the necessary data, as in previous chapters, and sets up the H2O cluster for analysis. We use the first 20,000 rows of data for training and the next 10,000 rows for testing. In addition to loading the data and setting up the H2O cluster, the data need to be transferred to H2O, which is done using the `as.h2o()` function:

```
## data and H2O setup
digits.train <- read.csv("train.csv")
digits.train$label <- factor(digits.train$label, levels = 0:9)

cl <- h2o.init(
  max_mem_size = "20G",
  nthreads = 10)

h2odigits <- as.h2o(
  digits.train,
  destination_frame = "h2odigits")

i <- 1:20000
h2odigits.train <- h2odigits[i, -1]

itest <- 20001:30000
h2odigits.test <- h2odigits[itest, -1]
xnames <- colnames(h2odigits.train)
```

For analysis, we use the `h2o.deeplearning()` function, which has many options and provides all the deep learning features available in H2O. Before we get into how to write the code for the model, however, a brief comment on reproducibility is in order. Often it is possible to set random seeds in order to make the results of running code exactly replicable. H2O uses a parallelization approach known as **Hogwild!**, that parallelizes stochastic gradient descent optimization, how the weights for the model are optimized/determined (see *Hogwild!: A Lock-Free Approach to Parallelizing Stochastic Gradient Descent* by *Niu, F., Recht, B., Ré, C.,* and *Wright, S. J.* (2011) at `https://www.eecs.berkeley.edu/~brecht/papers/hogwildTR.pdf`). Because of the way that Hogwild! works, it is not possible to make the results exactly replicable. Thus, when you run these codes, you may get slightly different results.

In the `h2o.deeplearning()` function call, the first argument is the list of x, or input, variable names. The training frame is the H2O dataset used for model training. The validation frame is only used to evaluate the performance of the model in data not trained on. Next we specify the activation function to use here: `"Tanh"`, which will be discussed in further detail in the next chapter on deep learning prediction. By setting the `autoencoder = TRUE` argument, the model is an auto-encoder model, rather than a regular model, so that no y or outcome variable(s) need to be specified.

Although we are using a deep learning function, to start with we use a single layer (shallow) of hidden neurons, with 50 hidden neurons. There are 20 training iterations, called **epochs**. The remaining arguments just specify not to use any form of regularization for this model. Regularization is not needed as there are hundreds of input variables and only 50 hidden neurons, so the relative simplicity of the model provides all the needed regularization. Finally, all the results are stored in an R object, `m1`:

```
m1 <- h2o.deeplearning(
  x = xnames,
  training_frame= h2odigits.train,
  validation_frame = h2odigits.test,
  activation = "Tanh",
  autoencoder = TRUE,
  hidden = c(50),
  epochs = 20,
  sparsity_beta = 0,
  input_dropout_ratio = 0,
  hidden_dropout_ratios = c(0),
  l1 = 0,
  l2 = 0
)
```

The remaining models are similar to the first model, m1, but adjust the complexity of the model by increasing the number of hidden neurons and adding regularization. Specifically, model m2a has no regularization, but increases the number of hidden neurons to 100. Model m2b uses 100 hidden neurons and also a sparsity beta of .5. Finally, model m2c uses 100 hidden neurons and a 20% dropout of the inputs (the x variables), which results in a form of *corrupted* inputs, so model m2c is a form of denoising auto-encoder:

```
m2a <- h2o.deeplearning(
  x = xnames,
  training_frame= h2odigits.train,
  validation_frame = h2odigits.test,
  activation = "Tanh",
  autoencoder = TRUE,
  hidden = c(100),
  epochs = 20,
  sparsity_beta = 0,
  input_dropout_ratio = 0,
  hidden_dropout_ratios = c(0),
  l1 = 0,
  l2 = 0
)


m2b <- h2o.deeplearning(
  x = xnames,
  training_frame= h2odigits.train,
  validation_frame = h2odigits.test,
  activation = "Tanh",
  autoencoder = TRUE,
  hidden = c(100),
  epochs = 20,
  sparsity_beta = .5,
  input_dropout_ratio = 0,
  hidden_dropout_ratios = c(0),
  l1 = 0,
```

```
   l2 = 0
)


m2c <- h2o.deeplearning(
   x = xnames,
   training_frame= h2odigits.train,
   validation_frame = h2odigits.test,
   activation = "Tanh",
   autoencoder = TRUE,
   hidden = c(100),
   epochs = 20,
   sparsity_beta = 0,
   input_dropout_ratio = .2,
   hidden_dropout_ratios = c(0),
   l1 = 0,
   l2 = 0
)
```

By typing the name of the stored model objects into R, we can get a summary of the model and its performance. To save space, much of the output has been omitted, but for each model the following output shows the performance as the **mean squared error (MSE)** in the training and validation data. A zero MSE indicates a perfect fit with higher values indicating deviations between $g(f(x))$ and x.

In model m1, the MSE is fairly low and identical in the training and validation data. This may be in part due to how relatively simple the model is (50 hidden neurons and 20 epochs, when there are hundreds of input variables). In model m2a, there is about a 45% reduction in the MSE, although both are low. However, with the greater model complexity, a slight difference between the training and validation metrics is observed. Similar results are noted in model m2b. Despite the fact that the validation metrics did not improve with regularization, the training metrics were closer to the validation metrics, suggesting the performance of the regularized training data generalizes better. In model m2c, the 20% input dropout without additional model complexity results in poorer performance in both the training and validation data. Our initial model with 100 hidden neurons is too simple still to really need much regularization:

m1

```
Training Set Metrics:
```

```
====================

MSE: (Extract with `h2o.mse`) 0.014


H2OAutoEncoderMetrics: deeplearning
** Reported on validation data. **


Validation Set Metrics:
====================

MSE: (Extract with `h2o.mse`) 0.014
```

m2a
```
Training Set Metrics:
====================

MSE: (Extract with `h2o.mse`) 0.0076


H2OAutoEncoderMetrics: deeplearning
** Reported on validation data. **


Validation Set Metrics:
====================

MSE: (Extract with `h2o.mse`) 0.0079
```

m2b
```
Training Set Metrics:
====================

MSE: (Extract with `h2o.mse`) 0.0077


H2OAutoEncoderMetrics: deeplearning
** Reported on validation data. **


Validation Set Metrics:
```

```
====================
```

MSE: (Extract with `h2o.mse`) 0.0079

m2c
Training Set Metrics:

```
====================
```

MSE: (Extract with `h2o.mse`) 0.0095

H2OAutoEncoderMetrics: deeplearning
** Reported on validation data. **

Validation Set Metrics:

```
====================
```

MSE: (Extract with `h2o.mse`) 0.0098

Another way we can look at the model results is to calculate how anomalous each case is. This can be done using the `h2o.anomaly()` function. The results are converted to data frames, labeled, and joined together in one final data table object called `error`:

```
error1 <- as.data.frame(h2o.anomaly(m1, h2odigits.train))
error2a <- as.data.frame(h2o.anomaly(m2a, h2odigits.train))
error2b <- as.data.frame(h2o.anomaly(m2b, h2odigits.train))
error2c <- as.data.frame(h2o.anomaly(m2c, h2odigits.train))

error <- as.data.table(rbind(
  cbind.data.frame(Model = 1, error1),
  cbind.data.frame(Model = "2a", error2a),
  cbind.data.frame(Model = "2b", error2b),
  cbind.data.frame(Model = "2c", error2c)))
```

Next we will use the data.table package to create a new data object, `percentile`, that contains the 99th percentile for each model:

```
percentile <- error[, .(
  Percentile = quantile(Reconstruction.MSE, probs = .99)
), by = Model]
```

Combining the information on how anomalous each case is and the 99th percentile, both by model, we can use the **ggplot2** package to plot the results. The histograms show the error rates for each case and the dashed line is the 99th percentile. Any value beyond the 99th percentile may be considered fairly extreme or anomalous:

```
p <- ggplot(error, aes(Reconstruction.MSE)) +
  geom_histogram(binwidth = .001, fill = "grey50") +
  geom_vline(aes(xintercept = Percentile), data = percentile, linetype =
2) +
  theme_bw() +
  facet_wrap(~Model)
print(p)
```

The results of this are shown in *Figure 4.3*. Models **2a** and **2b** have the lowest error rates, and you can see the small tails:

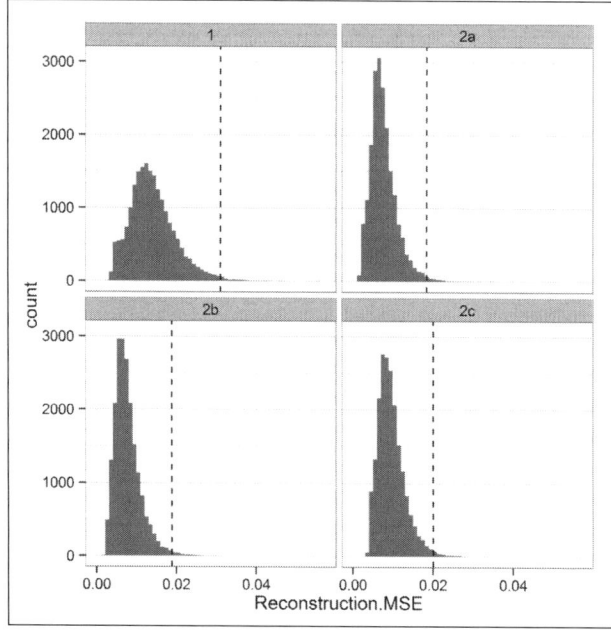

Figure 4.3

If we merge the data in wide form, with the anomaly values for each model in separate columns rather than in one long column with another indicating the model, we can plot the anomalous values against each other. The results are shown in *Figure 4.4*, and shows a high degree of correspondence between the models, with cases that tend to be anomalous for one model being anomalous for others as well:

```
error.tmp <- cbind(error1, error2a, error2b, error2c)
colnames(error.tmp) <- c("M1", "M2a", "M2b", "M2c")
plot(error.tmp)
```

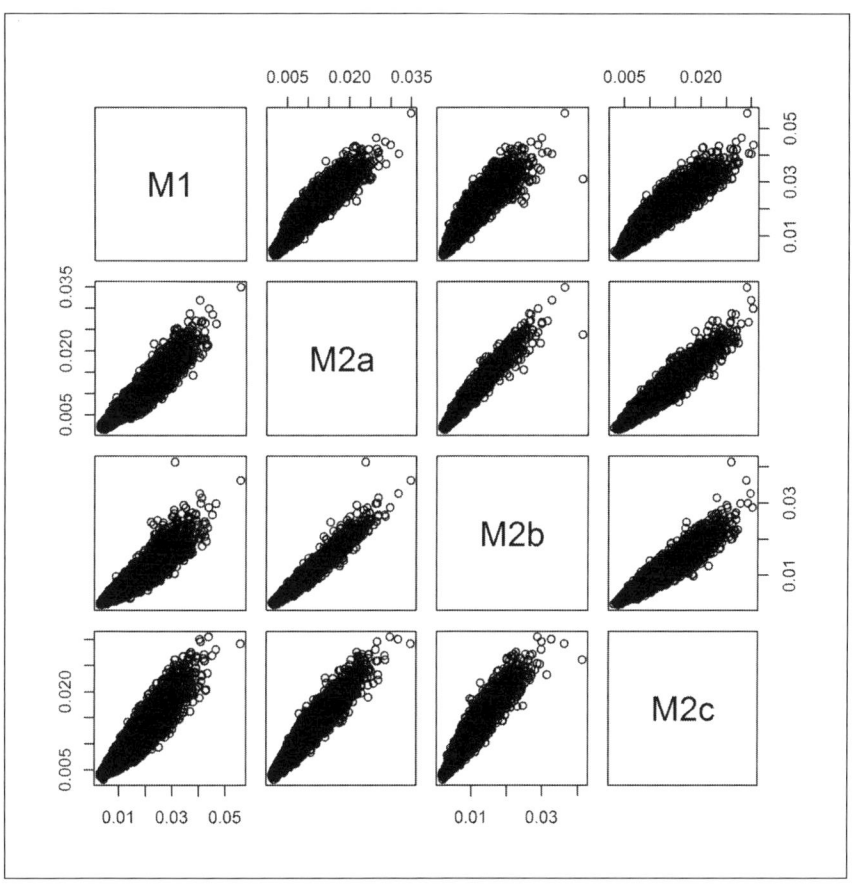

Figure 4.4

Another way we can examine the model results is to extract the deep features from the model. Deep features (layer by layer) can be extracted using the h2o.deepfeatures() function. The deep features are the values for the hidden neurons in the model. One way to explore these features is to correlate them and examine the distribution of correlations, again using the ggplot2 package, as shown in the following code. The results are shown in *Figure 4.5*. In general, the deep features have small correlations, r, with an absolute value < .20, with only very few having $|r| > .20$.

```
features1 <- as.data.frame(h2o.deepfeatures(m1, h2odigits.train))
r.features1 <- cor(features1)
r.features1 <- data.frame(r = r.features1[upper.tri(r.features1)])

p.hist <- ggplot(r.features1, aes(r)) +
  geom_histogram(binwidth = .02) +
  theme_classic()
print(p.hist)
```

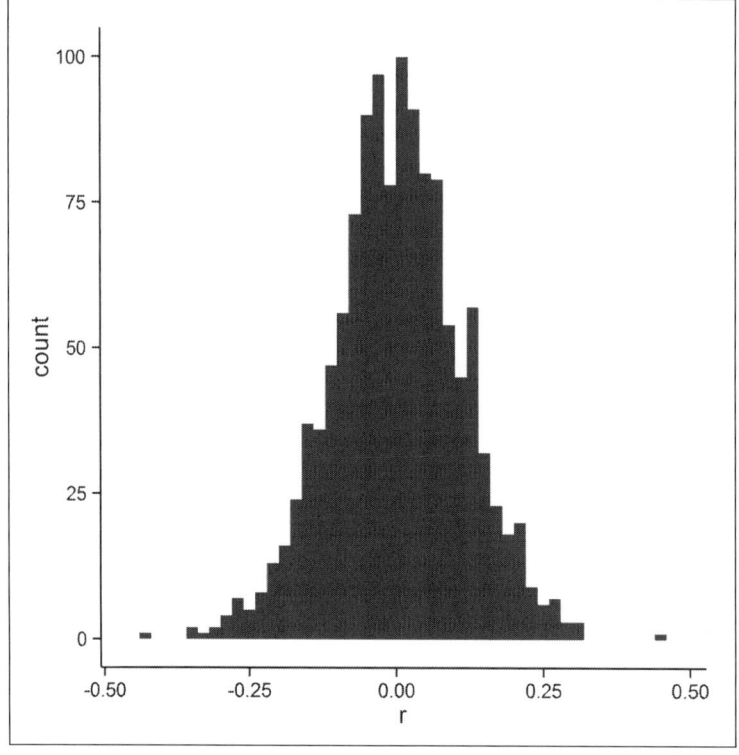

Figure 4.5

The examples so far show how auto-encoders can be trained, but have only represented shallow auto-encoders with a single hidden layer. We can also have deep auto-encoders with multiple hidden layers.

Given that we know the MNIST dataset consists of 10 different handwritten digits, perhaps we might try adding a second layer of hidden neurons with only 10 neurons, supposing that, when the model learns the features of the data, 10 prominent features may correspond to the 10 digits.

To add this second layer of hidden neurons, we pass a vector, `c(100, 10)`, to the `hidden` argument, and update the `hidden_dropout_ratios` argument as well, because a different dropout ratio can be used for each hidden layer:

```
m3 <- h2o.deeplearning(
  x = xnames,
  training_frame= h2odigits.train,
  validation_frame = h2odigits.test,
  activation = "Tanh",
  autoencoder = TRUE,
  hidden = c(100, 10),
  epochs = 30,
  sparsity_beta = 0,
  input_dropout_ratio = 0,
  hidden_dropout_ratios = c(0, 0),
  l1 = 0,
  l2 = 0
)
```

As we saw previously, we can extract the values for the hidden neurons. Here we again use the `h2o.deepfeatures()` function, but we specify that we want the values for layer 2. The first six rows of these features are shown next:

```
features3 <- as.data.frame(h2o.deepfeatures(m3, h2odigits.train, 2))
head(features3)
```

	DF.L2.C1	DF.L2.C2	DF.L2.C3	DF.L2.C4	DF.L2.C5	DF.L2.C6	DF.L2.C7
1	-0.16	0.01	0.61	0.610	0.7468	0.11	-0.3927
2	-0.28	-0.77	-0.82	0.563	-0.4422	-0.66	0.6042
3	-0.48	-0.23	0.24	-0.141	0.3252	0.42	-0.0088
4	-0.30	-0.37	0.42	-0.313	0.1896	-0.27	0.1442

5	-0.36	-0.73	-0.84	0.733	-0.4807	-0.62	0.6828
6	-0.24	0.16	-0.10	-0.037	-0.0064	-0.20	0.4794

	DF.L2.C8	DF.L2.C9	DF.L2.C10
1	0.023	-0.39	0.385
2	0.321	-0.39	-0.079
3	0.589	0.59	0.538
4	-0.224	-0.31	0.557
5	0.347	-0.62	-0.098
6	-0.592	0.11	0.253

Because there are no outcomes being predicted, these values are continuous and are not probabilities of there being a particular digit, but just values on 10 continuous hidden neurons.

Next we can add in the actual digit labels from the training data, and use the `melt()` function to reshape the data into a long dataset. From there, we can plot the means on each of the 10 hidden layers by which digit a case actually belongs to. If the 10 hidden features roughly correspond to the 10 digit labels, for particular labels (for example, 0, 3, etc.) they should have an extreme value on one deep feature, indicating the correspondence between a deep feature and the actual digits. The results are shown in *Figure 4.6*:

```
features3$label <- digits.train$label[i]
features3 <- melt(features3, id.vars = "label")


p.line <- ggplot(features3, aes(as.numeric(variable), value,
                    colour = label, linetype = label)) +
    stat_summary(fun.y = mean, geom = "line") +
    scale_x_continuous("Deep Features", breaks = 1:10) +
    theme_classic() +
    theme(legend.position = "bottom", legend.key.width = unit(1, "cm"))
print(p.line)
```

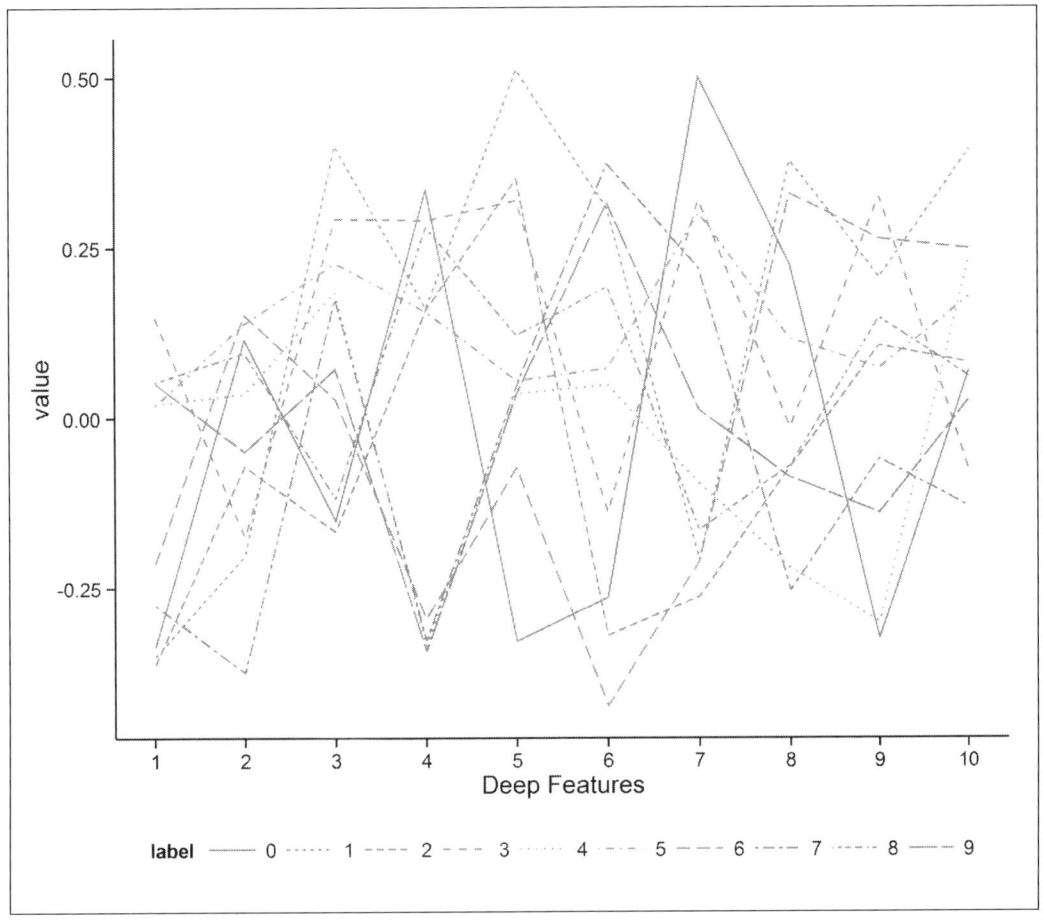

Figure 4.6

Although there does seem to be some correspondence (for example, zeros are particularly high on deep features **4** and **7**), in general the results are quite noisy without particularly clear indication of a high degree of separation between deep features and the actual digit labels.

Finally, we can take a look at the performance metrics for the model. With an MSE of about 0.039, the model fits substantially worse than did the shallow model, probably because having only 10 hidden neurons for the second layer is too simplistic to capture all the different features of the data needed to reproduce the original inputs:

m3

```
Training Set Metrics:
```

```
======================
```

```
MSE: (Extract with `h2o.mse`) 0.039
```

```
H2OAutoEncoderMetrics: deeplearning
** Reported on validation data. **
```

```
Validation Set Metrics:
======================
```

```
MSE: (Extract with `h2o.mse`) 0.04
```

This section has shown the basics of training an auto-encoder model, the code, and some ways of evaluating its performance. In the next section, we will examine a use case: finding anomalous values using an auto-encoder.

Use case – building and applying an auto-encoder model

For our use case, we are using the actigraphy data from smartphones we have previously examined. These data include actimetry on a number of individuals while sitting, standing, lying, walking, walking downstairs, and walking upstairs. Our goal is to identify any anomalous values or values that are aberrant or otherwise unusual.

To start with, we will load the training and testing data into R and then convert it over to H2O for analysis:

```
use.train.x <- read.table("UCI HAR Dataset/train/X_train.txt")
use.test.x <- read.table("UCI HAR Dataset/test/X_test.txt")

use.train.y <- read.table("UCI HAR Dataset/train/y_train.txt")[[1]]
use.test.y <- read.table("UCI HAR Dataset/test/y_test.txt")[[1]]

use.labels <- read.table("UCI HAR Dataset/activity_labels.txt")

h2oactivity.train <- as.h2o(
  use.train.x,
```

```
   destination_frame = "h2oactivitytrain")


h2oactivity.test <- as.h2o(
   use.test.x,
   destination_frame = "h2oactivitytest")
```

With the data in, we are ready to train our model. The setup is fairly similar to the initial models we trained. Here we use two layers with 100 hidden neurons each. For the moment, there is no specific regularization used, although again, given that there are significantly fewer hidden neurons than there are input variables, the model simplicity may provide adequate regularization:

```
mu1 <- h2o.deeplearning(
   x = colnames(h2oactivity.train),
   training_frame= h2oactivity.train,
   validation_frame = h2oactivity.test,
   activation = "Tanh",
   autoencoder = TRUE,
   hidden = c(100, 100),
   epochs = 30,
   sparsity_beta = 0,
   input_dropout_ratio = 0,
   hidden_dropout_ratios = c(0, 0),
   l1 = 0,
   l2 = 0
)
```

Examining the performance of the model, it has a very low reconstruction error. This suggests that the model is sufficiently complex to capture the key features of the data. There is no substantial difference in model performance between the training and validation data:

```
mu1
Training Set Metrics:
=====================


MSE: (Extract with `h2o.mse`) 0.001


H2OAutoEncoderMetrics: deeplearning
```

```
** Reported on validation data. **


Validation Set Metrics:

=====================


MSE: (Extract with `h2o.mse`) 0.0011
```

We can extract how anomalous each case is and plot the distribution. The results are shown in *Figure 4.7*. Clearly, there are a few cases that are far more anomalous than the rest, as shown by much higher error rates:

```
error1 <- as.data.frame(h2o.anomaly(mu1, h2oactivity.train))


pue1 <- ggplot(error1, aes(Reconstruction.MSE)) +
  geom_histogram(binwidth = .001, fill = "grey50") +
  geom_vline(xintercept = quantile(error1[[1]], probs = .99), linetype =
2) +
  theme_bw()
print(pue1)
```

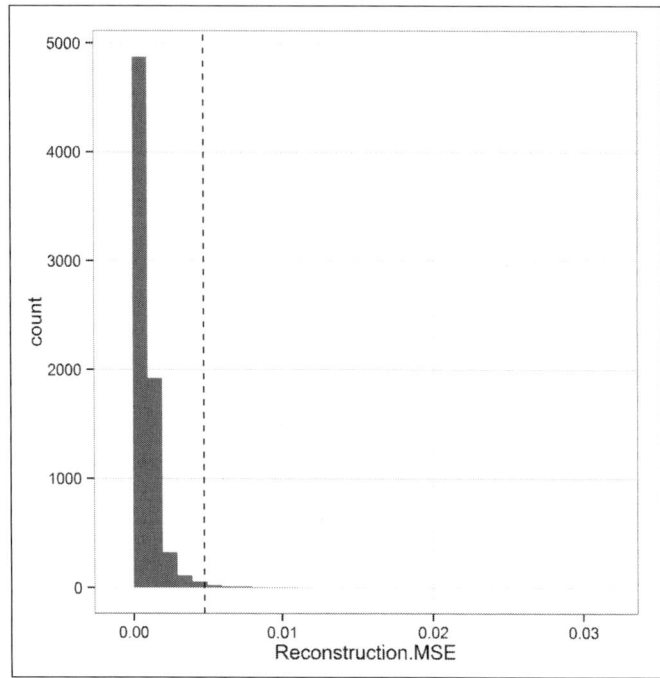

Figure 4.7

One way to try to explore these anomalous cases further is to examine whether any of the activities tend to have more or less anomalous values. We can do this by finding which cases are anomalous, here defined as the top 1% of error rates, and then extracting the activities of those cases and plotting them. The results from this are shown in *Figure 4.8*. The vast majority of anomalous cases come from walking downstairs or lying down. With a high error in recreating the inputs, the deep features may be a (relatively) poor representation of the input for those cases. In practice if we were classifying based on these results, we might want to exclude these cases as they do not seem to fit the features the model has learned:

```
i.anomolous <- errorul$Reconstruction.MSE >= quantile(errorul[[1]], probs
= .99)


pu.anomolous <- ggplot(as.data.frame(table(use.labels$V2[use.train.y[i.
anomolous]])),
       aes(Var1, Freq)) +
  geom_bar(stat = "identity") +
  xlab("") + ylab("Frequency") +
  theme_classic() +
  theme(axis.text.x = element_text(angle = 45, hjust = 1, vjust = 1))


# print the ggplot2 plot object
print(pu.anomolous)
```

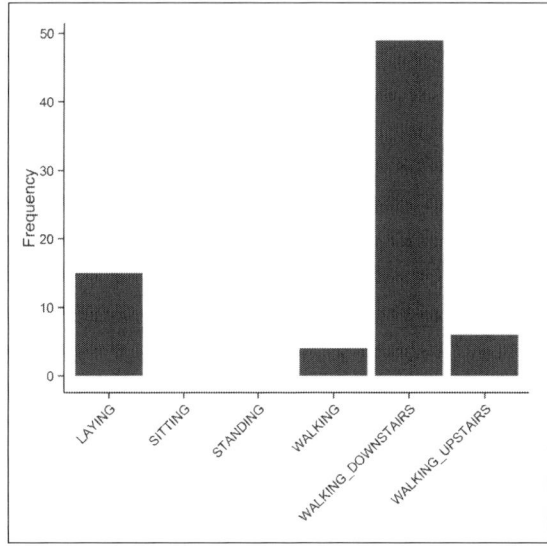

Figure 4.8

In this example, we used a deep auto-encoder model to learn the features of actimetry data from smartphones. Such work can be useful for excluding unknown or unusual activities, rather than incorrectly classifying them. For example, as part of an app that classifies what activity you engaged in for how many minutes, it may be better to simply leave out a few minutes where the model is uncertain or the hidden features do not adequately reconstruct the inputs, rather than to aberrantly call an activity walking or sitting when it was actually walking downstairs.

Such work can also help to identify where the model tends to have more issues. Perhaps further sensors and additional data are needed to represent walking downstairs or more could be done to understand why walking downstairs tends to produce relatively high error rates.

These deep auto-encoders are also useful in other contexts where identifying anomalies is important, such as with financial data or credit card usage patterns. Anomalous spending patterns may indicate fraud or that a credit card has been stolen. Rather than attempt to manually search through millions of credit card transactions, one could train an auto-encoder model and use it to identify anomalies for further investigation.

Fine-tuning auto-encoder models

In the previous sections of this chapter, we have learned how to train and use auto-encoder models. This last section explores how to optimize and fine-tune an auto-encoder model, examining issues such as how to pick the number of hidden neurons or the number of layers.

Sometimes, there may be conceptual reasons to assume certain structures about the data. However, if there are not, we may vary the values of these parameters to obtain the best model. One dilemma that is exacerbated when trying several models and choosing the best one is that, even if several models are equivalent, by chance in a given sample one may outperform the others. To combat this, we can use techniques such as cross-validation during training in order to optimize the parameter values while only using the training data, and then only this final model needs to be validated using the holdout or testing data. Currently, H2O does not support cross-validation for auto-encoder models. If we really wanted to use cross-validation, we could implement it manually. We can do this easily using the `createFolds()` function from the caret package:

```
## create 5 folds
folds <- createFolds(1:20000, k = 5)
```

Next we can create a list of the hyperparameters we want to try for tuning. We do this in the following code:

```
## create parameters to try
hyperparams <- list(
  list(
    hidden = c(50),
    input_dr = c(0),
    hidden_dr = c(0)),
  list(
    hidden = c(200),
    input_dr = c(.2),
    hidden_dr = c(0)),
  list(
    hidden = c(400),
    input_dr = c(.2),
    hidden_dr = c(0)),
  list(
    hidden = c(400),
    input_dr = c(.2),
    hidden_dr = c(.5)),
  list(
    hidden = c(400, 200),
    input_dr = c(.2),
    hidden_dr = c(.25, .25)),
  list(
    hidden = c(400, 200),
    input_dr = c(.2),
    hidden_dr = c(.5, .25)))
```

Finally, we can loop through the hyperparameters and 5-fold cross-validation to train all of the models. This may take several minutes to complete as we are training 6 x 5 or 30 models, some with hundreds of hidden neurons (note that, for this model to run with increased speed, we changed the H2O cluster to one with 12GB of memory and 5 cores):

```
fm <- lapply(hyperparams, function(v) {
  lapply(folds, function(i) {
  h2o.deeplearning(
```

```
    x = xnames,
    training_frame = h2odigits.train[-i, ],
    validation_frame = h2odigits.train[i, ],
    activation = "Tanh",
    autoencoder = TRUE,
    hidden = v$hidden,
    epochs = 30,
    sparsity_beta = 0,
    input_dropout_ratio = v$input_dr,
    hidden_dropout_ratios = v$hidden_dr,
    l1 = 0,
    l2 = 0
  )
 })
})
```

Next we loop through the results and extract the MSE for the *validation* data, which here is the single fold not used in the cross-validation:

```
fm.res <- lapply(fm, function(m) {
  sapply(m, h2o.mse, valid = TRUE)
})
```

We merge the results together into a data table to view and plot the performance across the folds of the cross-validation:

```
fm.res <- data.table(
  Model = rep(paste0("M", 1:6), each = 5),
  MSE = unlist(fm.res))


head(fm.res)
   Model         MSE
1:    M1 0.014619734
2:    M1 0.014655749
3:    M1 0.014651761
4:    M1 0.014310286
5:    M1 0.014303792
6:    M2 0.006781414
```

Finally, we can make boxplots of the results to see how spread out they are or if any of the cross-validated runs were especially aberrant. The results are shown in *Figure 4.9*, and it appears that the MSEs for each fold in the cross-validation are quite close so that the mean/median is a reasonable summary:

```
p.erate <- ggplot(fm.res, aes(Model, MSE)) +
  geom_boxplot() +
  stat_summary(fun.y = mean, geom = "point", colour = "red") +
  theme_classic()
print(p.erate)
```

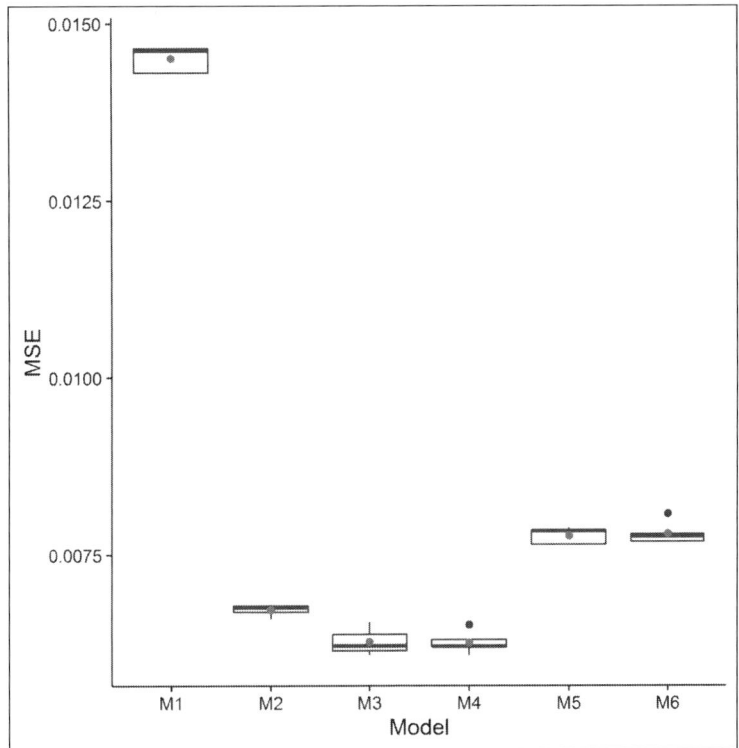

Figure 4.9

If we calculate the mean MSE by model and order from smallest to largest, these are the results we get:

```
fm.res[, .(Mean_MSE = mean(MSE)), by = Model][order(Mean_MSE)]
    Model    Mean_MSE
1:     M4 0.006261764
2:     M3 0.006276417
```

```
3:    M2 0.006725956
4:    M5 0.007768764
5:    M6 0.007797575
6:    M1 0.014508264
```

It appears that the fourth set of hyperparameters provided the lowest cross-validated MSE. The fourth set of hyperparameters was a fairly complex model, with 400 hidden neurons, but also had regularization with 20% of the input variables dropped and 50% of the hidden neurons dropped at each iteration, and this actually outperforms (albeit only slightly) the third set of hyperparameters where the same model complexity was used but without any dropout on the hidden layer. Although not much worse, the deep models here with a second layer of 200 hidden neurons perform worse than the shallow model.

With the best model selected, we can re-run using all training data and with our actual testing data, using the fourth set of hyperparameters:

```
fm.final <- h2o.deeplearning(
    x = xnames,
    training_frame = h2odigits.train,
    validation_frame = h2odigits.test,
    activation = "Tanh",
    autoencoder = TRUE,
    hidden = hyperparams[[4]]$hidden,
    epochs = 30,
    sparsity_beta = 0,
    input_dropout_ratio = hyperparams[[4]]$input_dr,
    hidden_dropout_ratios = hyperparams[[4]]$hidden_dr,
    l1 = 0,
    l2 = 0
)


fm.final
Training Set Metrics:
=====================


MSE: (Extract with `h2o.mse`) 0.005880221


H2OAutoEncoderMetrics: deeplearning
```

```
** Reported on validation data. **


Validation Set Metrics:

======================


MSE: (Extract with `h2o.mse`) 0.006072476
```

We can see that the MSE in our testing data, which was not used at all during training, is fairly close, though slightly worse than in the training data, and is actually slightly less than the MSE estimated from cross-validation, in this case. To the extent that we searched over a reasonable set of hyperparameters, this model is now optimized, validated, and ready for use.

In practice, it is often difficult to balance the tradeoff between the possibility of obtaining better performance with a different model or different set of hyperparameters with the time it takes to run and train many different models. Sometimes it can be helpful to explore the *optimal* model using a random subset of all data, if the data is very large, in order to speed computation. For this book, the example datasets we have been using are quite small compared to those commonly used in deep learning where there may be millions or hundreds of millions of cases and hundreds or thousands of variables or inputs. However, the approaches used here will scale to larger datasets, but will simply take more time. It is also worth noting that, though for these relatively small datasets we have been seeing good performance with fairly simpler models, larger datasets may benefit more from complex models and provide sufficient data to support learning a very complex structure.

Summary

This chapter introduced the distinction between supervised and unsupervised learning. It covered how to use unsupervised learning (such as auto-encoders) to learn the deep or hidden features of data. These hidden features may be used on their own, such as to better understand the structure of data, or for other applications. Two common applications of auto-encoders and unsupervised learning are to identify anomalous data (for example, outlier detection, financial fraud) and to pre-train more complex, often supervised, models such as deep neural networks. In the next chapter, we will learn how to train and build deep neural networks to develop prediction models (that is, supervised learning).

5
Training Deep Prediction Models

In this chapter we will explore how to train and build deep prediction models. We will focus on feedforward neural networks, which are perhaps the most common type and a good starting point.

This chapter will cover the following topics:

- Getting started with deep feedforward neural networks
- Common activation functions: rectifiers, hyperbolic tangent, and maxout
- Picking hyperparameters
- Training and predicting new data from a deep neural network
- Use case – training a deep neural network for automatic classification

In this chapter, we will not use any new packages. The only requirements are to source the `checkpoint.R` file to set up the R environment for the rest of the code shown and to initialize the H2O cluster. Both can be done using the following code:

```r
source("checkpoint.R")
options(width = 70, digits = 2)


cl <- h2o.init(
  max_mem_size = "12G",
  nthreads = 4)
```

Getting started with deep feedforward neural networks

A deep feedforward neural network is designed to approximate a function, $f()$, that maps some set of input variables, x, to an output variable, y. They are called **feedforward neural networks** because information flows from the inputs through each successive layer as far as the output, and there are no feedback or recursive loops (models including both forward and backward connections are referred to as **recurrent neural networks**).

Deep feedforward neural networks are applicable to a wide range of problems, and are particularly useful for applications such as image classification. More generally, feedforward neural networks are useful for prediction and classification where there is a clearly defined outcome (what digit an image contains, whether someone is walking upstairs or walking on a flat surface, the presence/absence of disease, and so on). In these cases, there is no particular need for a feedback loop. Recurrent networks are useful for cases where feedback loops are important, such as for natural language processing. However, these are outside the scope of this book, which will focus on training standard prediction models.

Deep feedforward neural networks can be constructed by chaining layers or functions together. For example, a network with four hidden layers is shown in *Figure 5.1*:

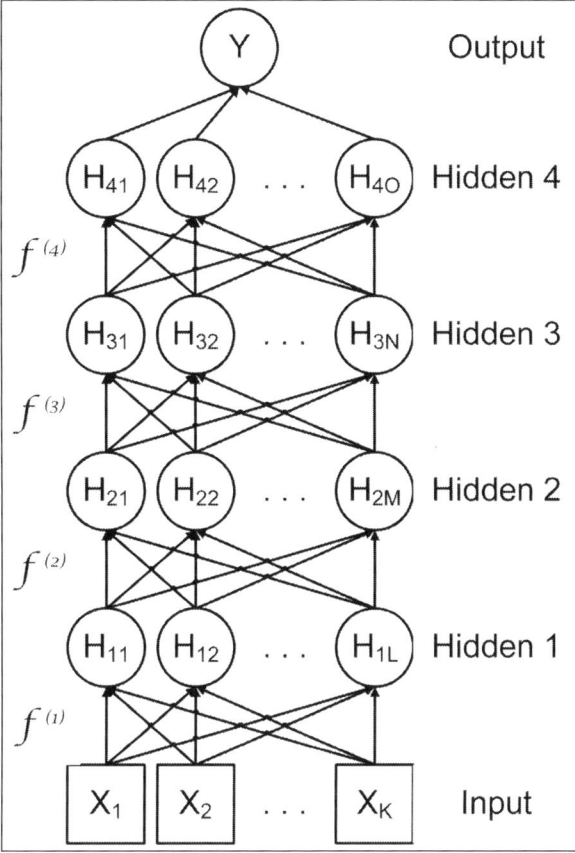

Figure 5.1

A different function is learned for each successive layer, and to finally map the hidden layers to the outcome. If sufficient hidden neurons are included in a layer, it can approximate to the desired degree of precision with many different types of functions. Even if the mapping from the final hidden layer to the outcome is a linear mapping with learned weights, feedforward neural networks can approximate non-linear functions, by first applying non-linear transformations from the input layer to the hidden layer. This is one of the key strengths of deep learning. In linear regression, for example, the model learns the weights from the inputs to the outcome. However, the functional form must be specified. In deep feedforward neural networks, the transformations from the input layer to the hidden layer are learned as well as the weights from the hidden layer to the outcome. In essence, the model learns the functional form as well as the weights. In practice, although it is unlikely that the model will learn the true generative model, it can (closely) approximate the true model. The more hidden neurons, the closer the approximation. Thus for practical, if not theoretically exact, purposes, the model learns the functional form.

Figure 5.1 shows a diagram of the model as a directed acyclic graph. Represented as a function, the overall mapping from the inputs, X, to the output, Y, is a multi-layered function. The first hidden layer is $H_1 = f^{(1)}(X, w_1, a_1)$, the second hidden layer is $H_2 = f^{(2)}(H_1, w_2, a_2)$, and so on. These multiple layers can allow complex functions and transformations to be built up from relatively simple ones.

The weights for each layer will be learned by the machine, but are also dependent on decisions made, such as how many hidden neurons should be in each layer and the activation function to be used, a topic explored further in the next section. Another key piece of the model that must be determined is the cost or loss function. The two most commonly used cost functions are **cross-entropy** and **mean squared error** (**MSE**), which is quadratic.

Common activation functions – rectifiers, hyperbolic tangent, and maxout

The activation function determines the mapping between inputs and a hidden layer. It defines the functional form for how a neuron gets activated. For example, a linear activation function could be defined as: $f(x) = x$, in which case the value for the neuron would be the raw input, x, times the learned weight, a linear model. A linear activation function is shown in the top panel of *Figure 5.2*. The problem with making activation functions linear is that this does not permit any non-linear functional forms to be learned. Previously, we have used the **hyperbolic tangent** as an activation function, so $f(x) = tanh(x)$. The hyperbolic tangent can work well in some cases, but a potential limitation is that, at either low or high values, it saturates, as shown in the middle panel of *Figure 5.2*.

Perhaps the most popular activation function currently, and a good first choice (*Nair, V.*, and *Hinton, G. E.* (2010)), is known as a **rectifier**. There can be different kinds of rectifiers but, most commonly, linear rectifiers are used and are defined by the function $f(x) = max(0, x)$. Linear rectifiers are flat below some threshold and are then linear; an example is shown in the bottom panel of *Figure 5.2*. Despite their simplicity, linear rectifiers provide a non-linear transformation, and enough linear rectifiers can be used to approximate arbitrary non-linear functions, unlike using only linear activation functions.

A final type of activation function we will discuss is **maxout** (*Goodfellow, I. J., Warde-Farley, D., Mirza, M., Courville, A.*, and *Bengio, Y.* (2013)). A maxout unit takes the maximum value of its inputs, although as usual this is after weighting so it is not the case that the input variable with the highest value will always *win*. Maxout activation functions seem to work particularly well with dropout.

For the purposes of this chapter, we will focus on linear rectifiers. This is both because they are a good default and perform well and also because we have already shown the use of hyperbolic tangent in previous chapters:

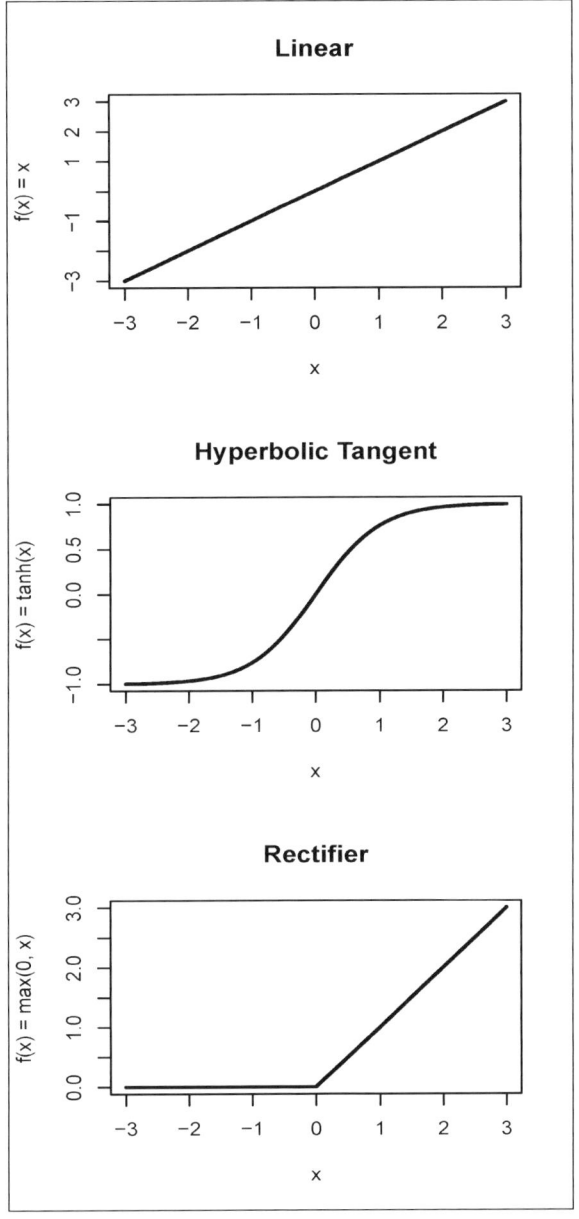

Figure 5.2

Picking hyperparameters

The parameters of a model typically refer to things such as the weights or bias/ intercept parameters. However, there are many other parameters that must be set at the offset and are not optimized or learned during model training. These are sometimes referred to as hyperparameters. Indeed, even the choice of model (for example, deep feedforward neural network, random forest, or support vector machine) can be seen as a hyperparameter.

Even if we assume that somehow we have decided that a deep feedforward neural network is the best modeling strategy, there are still many hyperparameters that must be set. These hyperparameters may be explicitly specified by the user or implicitly specified by using default values, where software provides them.

The values chosen for the hyperparameters can have a dramatic impact on the accuracy and training speed of a model. Indeed, we have already seen examples of trying different hyperparameters, such as trying different numbers of hidden neurons in a layer or a different number of layers. However, other hyperparameters also impact performance and speed. For example, in the following code, we set up the R environment, load the **Modified National Institute of Standards and Technology (MNIST)** data (images of handwritten digits) we have worked with, and run two prediction models, only varying the learning rate:

```
source("checkpoint.R")
options(width = 70, digits = 2)


cl <- h2o.init(
  max_mem_size = "12G",
  nthreads = 4)


## data setup
digits.train <- read.csv("train.csv")
digits.train$label <- factor(digits.train$label, levels = 0:9)


h2odigits <- as.h2o(
  digits.train,
  destination_frame = "h2odigits")


i <- 1:32000
h2odigits.train <- h2odigits[i, ]
```

```
itest <- 32001:42000
h2odigits.test <- h2odigits[itest, ]
xnames <- colnames(h2odigits.train)[-1]
```

```
system.time(ex1 <- h2o.deeplearning(
  x = xnames,
  y = "label",
  training_frame= h2odigits.train,
  validation_frame = h2odigits.test,
  activation = "RectifierWithDropout",
  hidden = c(100),
  epochs = 10,
  adaptive_rate = FALSE,
  rate = .001,
  input_dropout_ratio = 0,
  hidden_dropout_ratios = c(.2)
))
```

```
system.time(ex2 <- h2o.deeplearning(
  x = xnames,
  y = "label",
  training_frame= h2odigits.train,
  validation_frame = h2odigits.test,
  activation = "RectifierWithDropout",
  hidden = c(100),
  epochs = 10,
  adaptive_rate = FALSE,
  rate = .01,
  input_dropout_ratio = 0,
  hidden_dropout_ratios = c(.2)
))
```

The first difference is that ex1 took 1.34 times as long to train as did ex2. Printing each model shows a fairly large performance difference, as well. To save space in the book, most of the output from typing ex1 and ex2 is omitted and only the test set metrics are shown:

ex1

```
Test Set Metrics:

=======================

Metrics reported on full validation frame


MSE: (Extract with `h2o.mse`) 0.03326067

R^2: (Extract with `h2o.r2`) 0.9960457

Logloss: (Extract with `h2o.logloss`) 0.2021435

Confusion Matrix: Extract with `h2o.confusionMatrix(<model>, <data>)`)
```

	X0	X1	X2	X3	X4	X5	X6	X7	X8	X9	Error
0	984	0	1	0	0	3	13	2	6	2	0.02670623
1	0	1119	5	2	1	1	1	5	5	0	0.01755926
2	7	1	920	8	5	0	6	7	7	2	0.04465213
3	3	5	5	1006	1	13	1	7	7	1	0.04099142
4	0	7	3	0	896	2	5	2	4	13	0.03862661
5	6	2	4	17	5	835	7	1	10	5	0.06390135
6	5	2	1	0	6	8	966	1	2	0	0.02522704
7	2	2	8	7	3	1	0	1027	0	8	0.02930057
8	1	11	3	7	4	15	1	2	922	3	0.04850361
9	5	3	1	7	18	6	2	20	2	932	0.06425703
Totals	1013	1152	951	1054	939	884	1002	1074	965	966	0.03930000

ex2

```
Test Set Metrics:

=======================

Metrics reported on full validation frame
```

MSE: (Extract with `h2o.mse`) 0.1264212

R^2: (Extract with `h2o.r2`) 0.9849702

Logloss: (Extract with `h2o.logloss`) 2.136629

Confusion Matrix: Extract with `h2o.confusionMatrix(<model>, <data>)`)

```
================================================================
         X0    X1   X2   X3   X4    X5   X6    X7   X8   X9      Error
0       938     0    5   11    3    19   19     7    8    1 0.07220574
1         0  1105    6    6    2     6    1     8    5    0 0.02985075
2        18     7  757   54   20     9   47    36    5   10 0.21391485
3         1     2   22  887   10    36    0    50   30   11 0.15443279
4         1     7    0    1  854     7   13     8    5   36 0.08369099
5        11     6    4   45   16   767    8     5   29    1 0.14013453
6        13     5    5    1    6    63  887     5    6    0 0.10494450
7         2     8    3    3    4     7    0  1024    0    7 0.03213611
8         7    48   37   27    8    67   12    22  715   26 0.26212590
9         7     3    3   12   47    22    1   158   11  732 0.26506024
Totals  998  1191  842 1047  970  1003  988  1323  814  824 0.13340000
```

Although ex1 took longer to train, it performs substantially better on the test data than does ex2. The higher learning rate is faster but sacrifices performance. This highlights one of the decisions that needs to be made. However, as there are many hyperparameters, the decision about one is not made in isolation from the rest. One example of this is regularization. Often, relatively larger or more complex models are used with many hidden neurons and possibly multiple layers, choices that will tend to increase accuracy (at least within the training data) and reduce speed. However, these complex models often include some form of regularization, such as dropout, which would tend to reduce accuracy (at least within the training data) and improve speed as only a subset of neurons are included in any given iteration.

One of the most important decisions has to do with the architecture of the model. For example, decisions must be made as to how many layers there should be, how many hidden neurons should be in each layer, whether there should be any skipping patterns or each layer should only have sequential connections, and so on. Unfortunately, there are no simple rules to follow to resolve many of these questions. Good choices may rely on having a knowledge of the subject domain or prior analytical work may provide reasonable starting points.

In the absence of subject domain expertise or prior models, designing an effective architecture requires some trial and error. This trial and error can be a manual or an automated process. In theory, just as parameters are optimized, so hyperparameters could also be optimized. However, in practice this may not be feasible computationally as it can require running many variations of models, each of which requires substantial compute resources and time to complete.

Understanding what each hyperparameter does can help to inform your decisions. For example, if you start with a model and its performance is worse than is acceptable hyperparameters should be changed to allow greater capacity and flexibility in the model, for example, adding more hidden neurons, additional layers of hidden neurons, more training epochs, and so on. If there is a large difference between the model's performance on the training data and testing data, this may suggest the model is overfitting the data, in which case hyperparameters may be tweaked to reduce capacity or add more regularization. In some cases, it may be that more data is required to support fitting a more complex model needed to adequately predict the outcome. We will discuss some ways to refine model architecture (including more analytical approaches) in greater detail in *Chapter 6, Tuning and Optimizing Models.*

Training and predicting new data from a deep neural network

In this section we will learn how to train deep neural networks and use them to generate predictions on new data. The examples for this section will use the activity data we have worked with before, and the following code simply sets up the data:

```
use.train.x <- read.table("UCI HAR Dataset/train/X_train.txt")
use.test.x <- read.table("UCI HAR Dataset/test/X_test.txt")


use.train.y <- read.table("UCI HAR Dataset/train/y_train.txt")[[1]]
use.test.y <- read.table("UCI HAR Dataset/test/y_test.txt")[[1]]


use.train <- cbind(use.train.x, Outcome = factor(use.train.y))
use.test <- cbind(use.test.x, Outcome = factor(use.test.y))


use.labels <- read.table("UCI HAR Dataset/activity_labels.txt")
```

```
h2oactivity.train <- as.h2o(
   use.train,
   destination_frame = "h2oactivitytrain")


h2oactivity.test <- as.h2o(
   use.test,
   destination_frame = "h2oactivitytest")
```

We have already learned the components of training a deep prediction model. We use the `h2o.deeplearning()` function as we did for the auto-encoder models, but specify the variable names for both the *x* and *y* arguments. Before, we included the testing data to automatically get performance metrics on both training and testing data. However, to show how to generate predictions on new data, we do not include it in the call to `h2o.deeplearning()`. The activation function used is a linear rectifier with dropout both on the input variables (20%) and the hidden neurons (50%). This little example is a shallow network with only 50 hidden neurons and 10 training iterations. The cost (loss) function is cross-entropy:

```
mt1 <- h2o.deeplearning(
   x = colnames(use.train.x),
   y = "Outcome",
   training_frame= h2oactivity.train,
   activation = "RectifierWithDropout",
   hidden = c(50),
   epochs = 10,
   loss = "CrossEntropy",
   input_dropout_ratio = .2,
   hidden_dropout_ratios = c(.5), ,
   export_weights_and_biases = TRUE
)
```

We show the stored object by simply typing its name in the R console. The first information is about the type of model. The outcome has six discrete levels so a multinomial model is used. The model includes a total of 28,406 weights/biases. Biases are like intercepts or constant offsets. Because this is a feedforward neural network, there are only weights between adjacent layers. Input variables do not have biases, but hidden neurons and outcomes do. The 28,406 weights are made up from *561 * 50 = 28,050* weights between the input variables and the first layer of hidden neurons, *50 * 6 = 300* weights between the hidden neurons and the outcome (6 because there are different levels of the outcome), 50 biases for the hidden neurons, and 6 biases for the outcome.

The output also shows the number of layers and the number of units in each layer, the type of each unit, the dropout percentage, and other regularization and hyperparameter information:

mt1

```
Model Details:
==============


H2OMultinomialModel: deeplearning
Model ID:  DeepLearning_model_R_1451894068318_16
Status of Neuron Layers: predicting Outcome, 6-class classification,
multinomial distribution, CrossEntropy loss, 28,406 weights/biases, 406.9
KB, 73,520 training samples, mini-batch size 1
  layer units              type dropout        l1        l2 mean_rate
1     1   561              Input 20.00 %
2     2    50 RectifierDropout 50.00 % 0.000000 0.000000   0.001891
3     3     6             Softmax         0.000000 0.000000   0.004912
   rate_RMS momentum mean_weight weight_RMS mean_bias bias_RMS
1
2 0.002408 0.000000    0.000172   0.062088  0.347545 0.114483
3 0.015856 0.000000   -0.009241   0.755695 -0.029887 0.294392
```

The next set of output reports performance metrics on the training data, including the mean squared error (lower is better), R^2 (higher is better), and the log loss (lower is better):

```
H2OMultinomialMetrics: deeplearning
** Reported on training data. **
Description: Metrics reported on temporary (load-balanced) training frame


Training Set Metrics:
=====================
Metrics reported on temporary (load-balanced) training frame


MSE: (Extract with `h2o.mse`) 0.023
R^2: (Extract with `h2o.r2`) 0.99
Logloss: (Extract with `h2o.logloss`) 0.082
```

Finally, a confusion matrix is printed, which shows the actual outcome against the predicted outcome. The observed outcome is shown on the rows, and the predicted outcome is shown on the columns. The diagonal indicates correct classification, and the error rate by outcome level is shown:

```
Confusion Matrix: Extract with `h2o.confusionMatrix(<model>,train =
TRUE)`)
=====================================================================
          X1    X2  X3    X4    X5    X6  Error        Rate
1       1216    10   0     0     0     0 0.0082   10 / 1,226
2          3  1070   0     0     0     0 0.0028    3 / 1,073
3          2    11 973     0     0     0 0.0132   13 /   986
4          0     1   0  1236    40     9 0.0389   50 / 1,286
5          0     0   0   146  1228     0 0.1063  146 / 1,374
6          0     0   0     0     0  1407 0.0000    0 / 1,407
Totals  1221  1092 973  1382  1268  1416 0.0302  222 / 7,352


Hit Ratio Table: Extract with `h2o.hit_ratio_table(<model>,train = TRUE)`
=====================================================================
Top-6 Hit Ratios:
   k hit_ratio
1 1   0.969804
2 2   0.999728
3 3   1.000000
4 4   1.000000
5 5   1.000000
6 6   1.000000
```

We can extract and look at the features of the model using the h2o.deepfeatures() function, specifying the model, data, and layer we want to extract. The following code extracts features and looks at the first few rows. The outcome is also included by default. Note the zeros in the features; these are there because we used a linear rectifier, so values below zero are censored at zero:

```
f <- as.data.frame(h2o.deepfeatures(mt1, h2oactivity.train, 1))
f[1:10, 1:5]
```

	Outcome	DF.L1.C1	DF.L1.C2	DF.L1.C3	DF.L1.C4
1	5	0.00	5.9	0.091	2.1
2	5	0.00	4.7	0.000	1.7
3	5	0.00	4.4	0.102	1.5
4	5	0.00	4.9	0.000	1.9
5	5	0.00	5.0	0.000	1.8
6	5	0.00	4.9	0.000	2.0
7	5	0.00	4.9	0.000	1.6
8	5	0.00	4.6	0.000	1.8
9	5	0.00	5.0	0.000	1.6
10	5	0.13	5.1	0.000	1.3

Just as we extracted the features, we can extract weights from each layer. The following code extracts weights and makes a heatmap so we can see if there are any clear patterns of certain input variables having higher weights to particular hidden neurons:

```
w1 <- as.matrix(h2o.weights(mt1, 1))

## plot heatmap of the weights
tmp <- as.data.frame(t(w1))
tmp$Row <- 1:nrow(tmp)
tmp <- melt(tmp, id.vars = c("Row"))

p.heat <- ggplot(tmp,
        aes(variable, Row, fill = value)) +
  geom_tile() +
  scale_fill_gradientn(colours = c("black", "white", "blue")) +
  theme_classic() +
  theme(axis.text = element_blank()) +
  xlab("Hidden Neuron") +
  ylab("Input Variable") +
  ggtitle("Heatmap of Weights for Layer 1")
print(p.heat)
```

There does not seem to be any particularly clear pattern to the effect that particular neurons are made up predominantly of a few inputs as seen in the *Figure 5.3*:

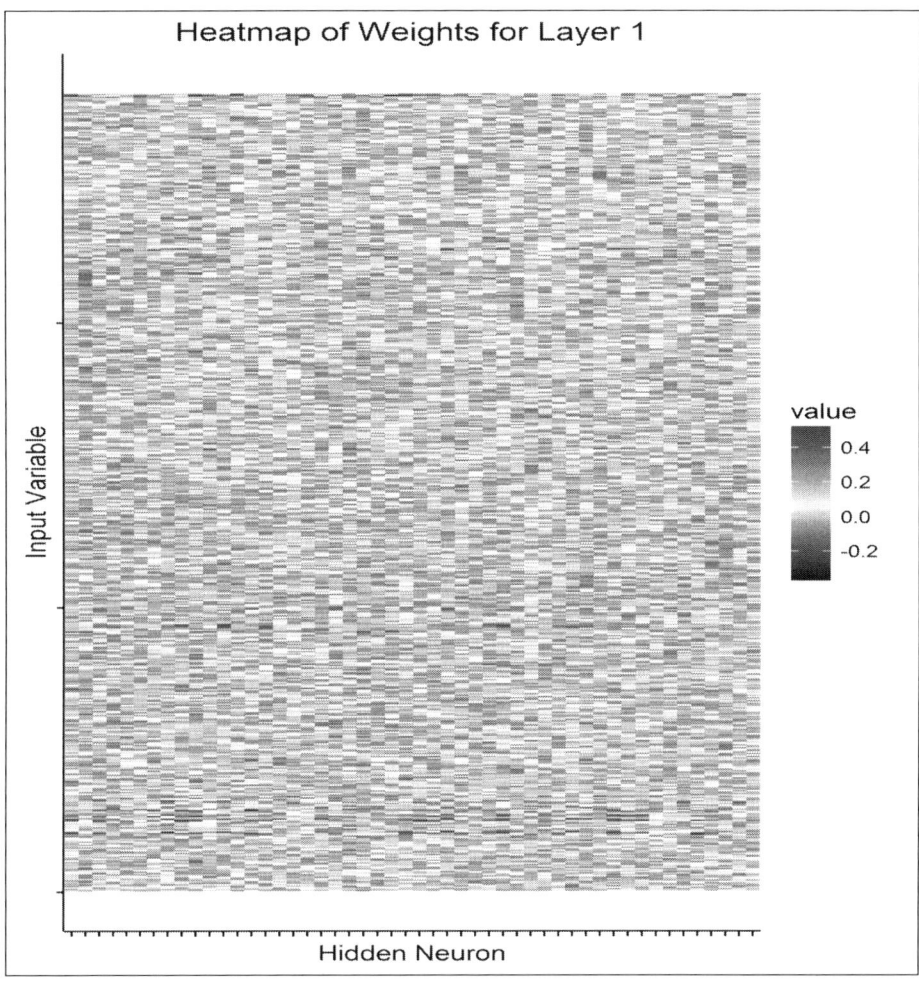

Figure 5.3

For all their complexity, once they are trained feedforward neural networks are straightforward to score and to use to generate predictions on data. There are built-in functions to do this, but to get a better understanding of the model we will work through one example manually.

As noted earlier, feedforward networks are constructed by *layering* functions together. We already extracted the weights for the first layer. However, in order to construct the neurons for hidden layer 1, we will also need the input data and the biases. Because we need to add the same constant term to an entire column to construct the deep features (even though the biases are stored as a vector with one bias for each hidden neuron), we replicate the biases and convert them into a matrix with dimensions matching the input data:

```
## input data
d <- as.matrix(use.train[, -562])


## biases for hidden layer 1 neurons
b1 <- as.matrix(h2o.biases(mt1, 1))
b12 <- do.call(rbind, rep(list(t(b1)), nrow(d)))
```

Now we can construct the features for layer 1, the hidden neurons. First, we need to standardize each column of the input data, which we can do by applying the scale() function in R to the data by columns (the second dimension of a matrix):

```
d.scaled <- apply(d, 2, scale)
```

Next we post multiply the scaled data by the weights we extracted earlier, and then add the bias matrix.

```
d.weighted <- d.scaled %*% t(w1) + b12
```

Because we included dropout on the hidden layer, we need to apply a correction. This is just a multiplicative correction based on the proportion of hidden units that are included at any iteration—that is: *1 – dropout proportion*:

```
d.weighted <- d.weighted * (1 - .5)
```

Finally, for each column, we only want to take values that are zero or higher, because we used a linear rectifier. We accomplish this in R by applying the pmax() function to the weighted data by columns:

```
d.weighted.rectifier <- apply(d.weighted, 2, pmax, 0)
```

We can check whether our work was correct by comparing it to the features extracted by H2O. We use the all.equal() function for comparison with some tolerance for slight numerical differences due to floating point arithmetic:

```
all.equal(
  as.numeric(f[, 2]),
```

```
    d.weighted.rectifier[, 1],
    check.attributes = FALSE,
    use.names = FALSE,
    tolerance = 1e-04)
```

In a similar fashion, we can extract the weights and biases for the next layer, which is the output layer. We create the predicted outcome just like we created the predicted hidden neurons, by multiplying by the weights and adding the biases. However, these operations are not applied to the raw data, but rather to the features we constructed in the first stage. As before, we need to expand the biases to the appropriate dimensions:

```
w2 <- as.matrix(h2o.weights(mt1, 2))
```

```
b2 <- as.matrix(h2o.biases(mt1, 2))
b22 <- do.call(rbind, rep(list(t(b2)), nrow(d)))
```

```
yhat <- d.weighted.rectifier %*% t(w2) + b22
```

To construct the hidden neurons, we used a linear rectifier activation function. For the outputs, a `softmax` function is used, which normalizes all the predictions to be within [0, 1] and ensures that they sum to one, like a predicted probability. We know to use the `softmax` function both because it is common and because, earlier in the model output, H2O indicated that `softmax` was the function linking to the output layer. The `softmax` function is defined for each case, and is the exponentiated predictions divided by the sum of the exponentiated predictions for that case:

```
yhat <- exp(yhat)
normalizer <- do.call(cbind, rep(list(rowSums(yhat)), ncol(yhat)))
yhat <- yhat / normalizer
```

Finally, we can derive a predicted classification by choosing the output column with the highest predicted probability, using the `which.max()` function, and append this to our prediction dataset:

```
yhat <- cbind(Outcome = apply(yhat, 1, which.max), yhat)
```

Via the `h2o.predict()` function, we can also extract predictions using the built-in function, and we can compare these with the predictions we generated manually:

```
yhat.h2o <- as.data.frame(h2o.predict(mt1, newdata = h2oactivity.train))


xtabs(~ yhat[, 1] + yhat.h2o[, 1])


        yhat.h2o[, 1]
yhat[, 1]     1     2     3     4     5     6
      1 1216     0     0     0     0     0
      2    0  1122     0     0     0     0
      3    0     0   948     0     0     0
      4    0     0     0  1316     0     0
      5    0     0     0     0  1344     0
      6    0     0     0     0     0  1406
```

Our manual process matches that of H2O exactly. Of course, in practice one would not re-implement the prediction function manually, and the code that demonstrates doing it manually is not particularly computationally efficient. However, working through examples like this can help to clarify exactly what pieces go into the model and how they are used. If we had many hidden layers of neurons, the process would be very similar, just repeating the steps to generate features for each layer, and always building on top of the results from the previous layer.

Use case – training a deep neural network for automatic classification

For our use case, we use data from a subset of the **Million Song Dataset**, from the University of California Irvine online dataset repository (*Lichman, M.* (2013)). There are 515,345 cases, with the first 463,715 being training cases and the last 51,630 cases used for testing. The first column of the dataset contains the year and the remaining columns are features from the timbre of the song. Download and decompress the data from here: `http://archive.ics.uci.edu/ml/datasets/YearPredictionMSD`. Our goal is to predict the year each song was released.

First we need to download the data and then unzip it, which we can do using the following code:

```
download.file(
"http://archive.ics.uci.edu/ml/machine-learning-databases/00203/
YearPredictionMSD.txt.zip", destfile = "YearPredictionMSD.txt.zip")
```

```
unzip("YearPredictionMSD.txt.zip")
```

Now we can read data into R using `fread()` from the **data.table** package. The `fread()` function is preferable to `read.csv()` here because it can be orders-of-magnitude faster, and it still took 30 seconds on a high-end desktop with a solid state hard drive:

```
d <- fread("YearPredictionMSD.txt", sep = ",")
```

First we can take a quick look at the distribution of the outcome, the year of release. The following code creates a histogram that is shown in *Figure 5.4*:

```
p.hist <- ggplot(d[, .(V1)], aes(V1)) +
  geom_histogram(binwidth = 1) +
  theme_classic() +
  xlab("Year of Release")
print(p.hist)
```

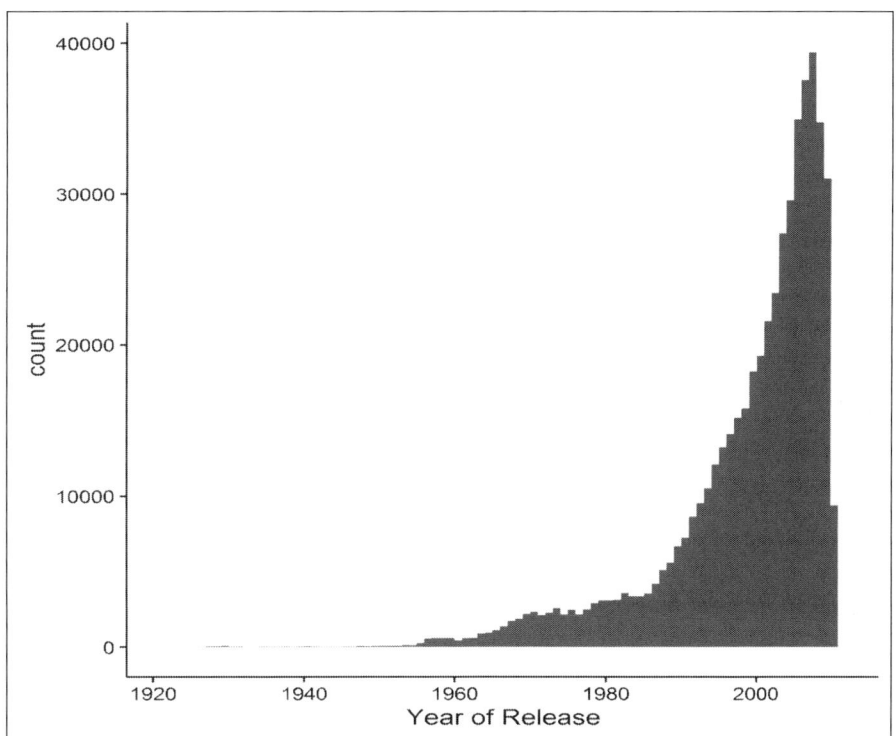

Figure 5.4

One possible concern is that the relatively extreme values may exert an undue influence on the model. We can reduce this by reflecting the distribution and taking the square root. We could also exclude a small amount of the more extreme cases, such as by excluding the bottom and top 0.5% (1% of data total). Checking the quantiles (in the following code) would include the years 1957 to 2010:

```
quantile(d$V1, probs = c(.005, .995))
0.5% 100%
1957 2010
```

The following code trims the data and converts the training and testing datasets for H2O:

```
d.train <- d[1:463715][V1 >= 1957 & V1 <= 2010]


d.test <- d[463716:515345][V1 >= 1957 & V1 <= 2010]


h2omsd.train <- as.h2o(
   d.train,
   destination_frame = "h2omsdtrain")


h2omsd.test <- as.h2o(
   d.test,
   destination_frame = "h2omsdtest")
```

To get started and provide some baseline performance levels, we can build a linear regression model:

```
summary(m0 <- lm(V1 ~ ., data = d.train))$r.squared
[1] 0.24

cor(
   d.test$V1,
   predict(m0, newdata = d.test))^2
[1] 0.23
```

Although not great, linear regression accounts for 24% of the variance in years in the training data and 23% in the testing data; these results provide a benchmark for us to beat with the feedforward neural network.

Our first network is shallow with a single hidden layer and is fairly small. This is a larger dataset than some of the previous ones we have worked with, but it is still small enough that it is easy to work with all of it. To make performance scoring occur on the full dataset, we use the special value, 0, passed to the `score_training_samples` and `score_validation_samples` arguments. On the 10-core H2O cluster setup, the model took 79 seconds to train, recorded using the `system.time()` function:

```
m1 <- h2o.deeplearning(
  x = colnames(d)[-1],
  y = "V1",
  training_frame= h2omsd.train,
  validation_frame = h2omsd.test,
  activation = "RectifierWithDropout",
  hidden = c(50),
  epochs = 100,
  input_dropout_ratio = 0,
  hidden_dropout_ratios = c(0),
  score_training_samples = 0,
  score_validation_samples = 0,
  diagnostics = TRUE,
  export_weights_and_biases = TRUE,
  variable_importances = TRUE
  )
```

The results from this simple model show a marked improvement over the linear regression model. The feedforward neural network, even though it only had a single layer with 50 hidden neurons, accounted for 32% of the variance in release year in the testing data, up from 23% using only linear regression.

Because the model was small and had fewer hidden neurons than input variables, no dropout or other regularization was used. However, the performance discrepancy between the training and testing data ($R^2 = 0.37$ versus $R^2 = 0.32$, respectively), indicates that some regularization may be helpful:

```
m1
```

```
Model Details:
==============
```

```
H2ORegressionModel: deeplearning
Model ID:  DeepLearning_model_R_1451972322936_5
Status of Neuron Layers: predicting V1, regression, gaussian
distribution, Quadratic loss, 4,601 weights/biases, 72.5 KB, 13,702,476
training samples, mini-batch size 1
```

	layer	units	type	dropout	l1	l2	mean_rate
1	1	90	Input	0.00 %			
2	2	50	RectifierDropout	0.00 %	0.000000	0.000000	0.009403
3	3	1	Linear		0.000000	0.000000	0.000218

	rate_RMS	momentum	mean_weight	weight_RMS	mean_bias	bias_RMS
1						
2	0.007939	0.000000	-0.018219	0.598229	-2.199141	2.245173
3	0.000202	0.000000	-0.042807	0.103305	-0.767868	0.000000

```
H2ORegressionMetrics: deeplearning
** Reported on training data. **
Description: Metrics reported on full training frame


MSE:  76
R2 :  0.37
Mean Residual Deviance :  76



H2ORegressionMetrics: deeplearning
** Reported on validation data. **
Description: Metrics reported on temporary (load-balanced) validation
frame


MSE:  80
R2 :  0.32
Mean Residual Deviance :  80
```

Although our shallow neural network model was an improvement over linear regression, it still did not perform well and there is clearly room for improvement. Next, we will try a larger, deep feedforward neural network. In the model code next, we have three layers of hidden neurons, with 200, 200, and 400 hidden neurons, respectively. We will also introduce a modest amount of dropout on the hidden (but not input) layer. This model took 843 seconds to train:

```
m2 <- h2o.deeplearning(
  x = colnames(d)[-1],
  y = "V1",
  training_frame= h2omsd.train,
  validation_frame = h2omsd.test,
  activation = "RectifierWithDropout",
  hidden = c(200, 200, 400),
  epochs = 100,
  input_dropout_ratio = 0,
  hidden_dropout_ratios = c(.2, .2, .2),
  score_training_samples = 0,
  score_validation_samples = 0,
  diagnostics = TRUE,
  export_weights_and_biases = TRUE,
  variable_importances = TRUE
  )
```

Examining the performance of the model shows a noticeable improvement from the small and shallow model we tried first. In the testing data, the shallow model had an R^2 of 0.32 whereas the deep model has an R^2 of 0.35.

There is also a degree of overfitting. The difference in R^2 between the training and testing data is 0.05, which is comparable to the simpler model where the difference was also 0.05. The more complex model improves performance, with little difference in overfitting, perhaps due to the dropout used:

m2

```
Model Details:
==============
```

H2ORegressionModel: deeplearning

Model ID: DeepLearning_model_R_1452031055473_5

Status of Neuron Layers: predicting V1, regression, gaussian distribution, Quadratic loss, 139,201 weights/biases, 1.6 MB, 22,695,351 training samples, mini-batch size 1

	layer	units	type	dropout	l1	l2	mean_rate
1	1	90	Input	0.00 %			
2	2	200	RectifierDropout	20.00 %	0.000000	0.000000	0.011513
3	3	200	RectifierDropout	20.00 %	0.000000	0.000000	0.014861
4	4	400	RectifierDropout	20.00 %	0.000000	0.000000	0.054338
5	5	1	Linear		0.000000	0.000000	0.001258

	rate_RMS	momentum	mean_weight	weight_RMS	mean_bias	bias_RMS
1						
2	0.004978	0.000000	0.000848	0.207373	-0.254659	0.321144
3	0.012359	0.000000	-0.032566	0.104347	1.017329	0.341556
4	0.036596	0.000000	-0.031768	0.072171	0.651546	0.292565
5	0.000505	0.000000	0.001421	0.020867	-0.596303	0.000000

H2ORegressionMetrics: deeplearning

** Reported on training data. **

Description: Metrics reported on full training frame

MSE: 66

R2 : 0.40

Mean Residual Deviance : 66

H2ORegressionMetrics: deeplearning

** Reported on validation data. **

Description: Metrics reported on temporary (load-balanced) validation frame

MSE: 70

R2 : 0.35

Mean Residual Deviance : 70

To see whether the performance on the testing data can be improved further, we will try one additional model including substantially more hidden neurons in each layer, more training iterations (epochs), and with a higher degree of regularization. Readers may not wish to run the following code (the model took over 10 hours to complete on the 10-core H2O cluster):

```
m3 <- h2o.deeplearning(
  x = colnames(d)[-1],
  y = "V1",
  training_frame= h2omsd.train,
  validation_frame = h2omsd.test,
  activation = "RectifierWithDropout",
  hidden = c(500, 500, 1000),
  epochs = 500,
  input_dropout_ratio = 0,
  hidden_dropout_ratios = c(.5, .5, .5),
  score_training_samples = 0,
  score_validation_samples = 0,
  diagnostics = TRUE,
  export_weights_and_biases = TRUE
  )
```

The performance of this model on the testing data was actually worse than either of the previous two models, though still superior to the linear regression:

m3

```
Model Details:
==============


H2ORegressionModel: deeplearning
Model ID:  DeepLearning_model_R_1451972322936_15
Status of Neuron Layers: predicting V1, regression, gaussian
distribution, Quadratic loss, 798,001 weights/biases, 9.2 MB, 47,002,720
training samples, mini-batch size 1
```

	layer	units	type	dropout	l1	l2	mean_rate
1	1	90	Input	0.00 %			
2	2	500	RectifierDropout	50.00 %	0.000000	0.000000	0.028872

3	3	500	RectifierDropout	50.00 %	0.000000	0.000000	0.047632
4	4	1000	RectifierDropout	50.00 %	0.000000	0.000000	0.084886
5	5	1	Linear		0.000000	0.000000	0.001238

	rate_RMS	momentum	mean_weight	weight_RMS	mean_bias	bias_RMS
1						
2	0.014727	0.000000	0.000941	0.069018	0.417255	0.048082
3	0.020226	0.000000	-0.007515	0.049535	0.968111	0.054521
4	0.062396	0.000000	-0.009451	0.038735	0.929930	0.032726
5	0.000445	0.000000	0.000538	0.014785	-0.478095	0.000000

H2ORegressionMetrics: deeplearning

** Reported on training data. **

Description: Metrics reported on full training frame

MSE: 84

R2 :   0.30

Mean Residual Deviance :   84

H2ORegressionMetrics: deeplearning

** Reported on validation data. **

Description: Metrics reported on temporary (load-balanced) validation frame

MSE: 85

R2 :   0.28

Mean Residual Deviance :   85

Our best model then is still the deep model, but with fewer hidden neurons per layer. One way that we can try to see if that model can be improved is to try training for additional epochs or iterations. In the model output, there is a model ID. For the best performing model, this was: `DeepLearning_model_R_1452031055473_5`. This can be passed to the `checkpoint` argument of the `h2o.deeplearning()` function so that training begins using the weights from the previous model. Note that the model ID will be different every time you run the code; thus, when running it on your own computer or servers, you will need to use the model ID from your run.

As long as the general architecture—the number of hidden neurons, layers, and connections—remains the same, using the checkpoint can be a great time saver. This is not only true because the previous training iterations can be re-used, but also because it tends to take longer for earlier than later iterations. The following example shows how to run the model, changing the epochs from 500 to 1,000 (since 500 have already been done) and starting from the previous model run by specifying the model name as a character string to the `checkpoint` argument:

```
m2b <- h2o.deeplearning(
  x = colnames(d)[-1],
  y = "V1",
  training_frame= h2omsd.train,
  validation_frame = h2omsd.test,
  activation = "RectifierWithDropout",
  hidden = c(200, 200, 400),
  checkpoint = "DeepLearning_model_R_1452031055473_5",
  epochs = 1000,
  input_dropout_ratio = 0,
  hidden_dropout_ratios = c(.2, .2, .2),
  score_training_samples = 0,
  score_validation_samples = 0,
  diagnostics = TRUE,
  export_weights_and_biases = TRUE,
  variable_importances = TRUE


)
```

However, in the end, the additional epochs did not improve the model performance. In fact, it became slightly worse:

m2b

```
Model Details:
==============


H2ORegressionModel: deeplearning
Model ID:  DeepLearning_model_R_1452031055473_81
```

Status of Neuron Layers: predicting V1, regression, gaussian distribution, Quadratic loss, 139,201 weights/biases, 1.6 MB, 30,054,531 training samples, mini-batch size 1

	layer	units	type	dropout	l1	l2	mean_rate
1	1	90	Input	0.00 %			
2	2	200	RectifierDropout	20.00 %	0.000000	0.000000	0.008598
3	3	200	RectifierDropout	20.00 %	0.000000	0.000000	0.012581
4	4	400	RectifierDropout	20.00 %	0.000000	0.000000	0.025138
5	5	1	Linear		0.000000	0.000000	0.000895

	rate_RMS	momentum	mean_weight	weight_RMS	mean_bias	bias_RMS
1						
2	0.004485	0.000000	-0.004116	0.473692	-1.601533	1.060434
3	0.017790	0.000000	-0.040249	0.239924	0.767950	1.305716
4	0.022843	0.000000	-0.048592	0.105753	0.360921	0.439503
5	0.000582	0.000000	-0.001778	0.029287	-0.065273	0.000000

H2ORegressionMetrics: deeplearning

** Reported on training data. **

Description: Metrics reported on full training frame

MSE: 62

R2 : 0.43

Mean Residual Deviance : 62

H2ORegressionMetrics: deeplearning

** Reported on validation data. **

Description: Metrics reported on temporary (load-balanced) validation frame

MSE: 72

R2 : 0.33

Mean Residual Deviance : 72

Working with model results

It is easy to save models in R but, when calling H2O from R, most results are not actually stored in R; instead they are stored in the H2O cluster. Thus, only saving the R object will merely save the reference to the model in the H2O cluster and, if that is shut down and lost, the full model results will not be saved. To avoid this and save the full model results, we use the `h2o.saveModel()` function and specify the model to be saved (by passing the R object), the `path`, and whether to overwrite files if already there (using `force = TRUE`):

```
h2o.saveModel(
   object = m2,
   path = "c:\\Users\\jwile\\DeepLearning",
   force = TRUE)
```

This will create a directory with all of the files needed to load and use the model again. Once you have saved a model, you can load it back into a new H2O cluster using the `h2o.loadModel()` function. Note that you also must specify the folder name for the model results to load.

In addition to just saving the model results to be loaded again into an H2O cluster, models can be saved as a **Plain Old Java Object (POJO)**. Saving models as a POJO is useful as they can be embedded in other applications and used to score results. H2O models can be saved as a POJO using the `h2o.download_pojo()` function, with the same arguments.

Another useful function is `h2o.scoreHistory()`. The score history shows the performance of the model across iterations as well as a time stamp and the duration for each epoch. The following code shows how to use it and the results:

```
h2o.scoreHistory(m2)
```

```
Scoring History:
               timestamp            duration training_speed     epochs
1   2016-01-06 23:20:18     0.000 sec                        0.00000
2   2016-01-06 23:20:26    15.537 sec 13922 rows/sec   0.21687
3   2016-01-06 23:21:51  1 min 40.761 sec 22603 rows/sec   4.11902
4   2016-01-06 23:23:15  3 min  4.790 sec 25030 rows/sec   8.66890
5   2016-01-06 23:24:39  4 min 28.208 sec 26347 rows/sec  13.43506
6   2016-01-06 23:26:00  5 min 49.401 sec 27540 rows/sec  18.41458
```

```
7  2016-01-06 23:27:21  7 min 10.032 sec 28317 rows/sec 23.39553
8  2016-01-06 23:28:40  8 min 29.325 sec 28928 rows/sec 28.37323
9  2016-01-06 23:29:59  9 min 48.908 sec 29354 rows/sec 33.34907
10 2016-01-06 23:31:21 11 min 10.056 sec 29771 rows/sec 38.54472
11 2016-01-06 23:32:41 12 min 30.532 sec 30130 rows/sec 43.73626
12 2016-01-06 23:34:04 13 min 53.652 sec 30444 rows/sec 49.14818
13 2016-01-06 23:34:12 14 min  1.667 sec 30442 rows/sec 49.14818
```

	iterations	samples	training_MSE	training_deviance
1	0	0.000000		
2	1	100145.000000	73.50950	73.50950
3	19	1902057.000000	65.90201	65.90201
4	40	4003071.000000	66.39865	66.39865
5	62	6203960.000000	63.97995	63.97995
6	85	8503375.000000	65.20361	65.20361
7	108	10803448.000000	62.67372	62.67372
8	131	13102020.000000	63.91678	63.91678
9	154	15399734.000000	60.31355	60.31355
10	178	17798949.000000	60.15803	60.15803
11	202	20196268.000000	61.71012	61.71012
12	227	22695351.000000	58.34747	58.34747
13	227	22695351.000000	65.90201	65.90201

	training_r2	validation_MSE	validation_deviance	validation_r2
1				
2	0.32564	73.67272	73.67272	0.30763
3	0.39543	69.57711	69.57711	0.34612
4	0.39087	71.70615	71.70615	0.32611
5	0.41306	70.45211	70.45211	0.33790
6	0.40184	71.98921	71.98921	0.32345

7	0.42505	70.90519	70.90519	0.33364
8	0.41364	72.69913	72.69913	0.31678
9	0.44670	70.49905	70.49905	0.33746
10	0.44812	70.76801	70.76801	0.33493
11	0.43389	72.22494	72.22494	0.32124
12	0.46473	70.55234	70.55234	0.33696
13	0.39543	69.57711	69.57711	0.34612

So far we have only examined the overall performance of the model. Although this is a useful summary, it provides less than a complete picture. Examining the model residuals can help us understand whether the model performs consistently across the range of the data and any anomalous residuals; it also helps us to generally assess performance more comprehensively. We can calculate residuals by getting predicted values for all cases using the h2o.predict() function and then taking the difference between the observed values and the predictions. The following code extracts predictions, joins them with observed values, and plots them. A residual of zero indicates a perfect prediction, with either positive or negative residuals indicating over- or under-prediction. Since years are discrete, we can visualize the data using boxplots of the residuals for each actual year of song release, using the following code. This is shown in *Figure 5.5*:

```
yhat <- as.data.frame(h2o.predict(m1, h2omsd.train))
yhat <- cbind(as.data.frame(h2omsd.train[["V1"]]), yhat)

p.resid <- ggplot(yhat, aes(factor(V1), predict - V1)) +
  geom_boxplot() +
  geom_hline(yintercept = 0) +
  theme_classic() +
  theme(axis.text.x = element_text(
        angle = 90, vjust = 0.5, hjust = 0)) +
  xlab("Year of Release") +
```

```
    ylab("Predicted Year of Release")
print(p.resid)
```

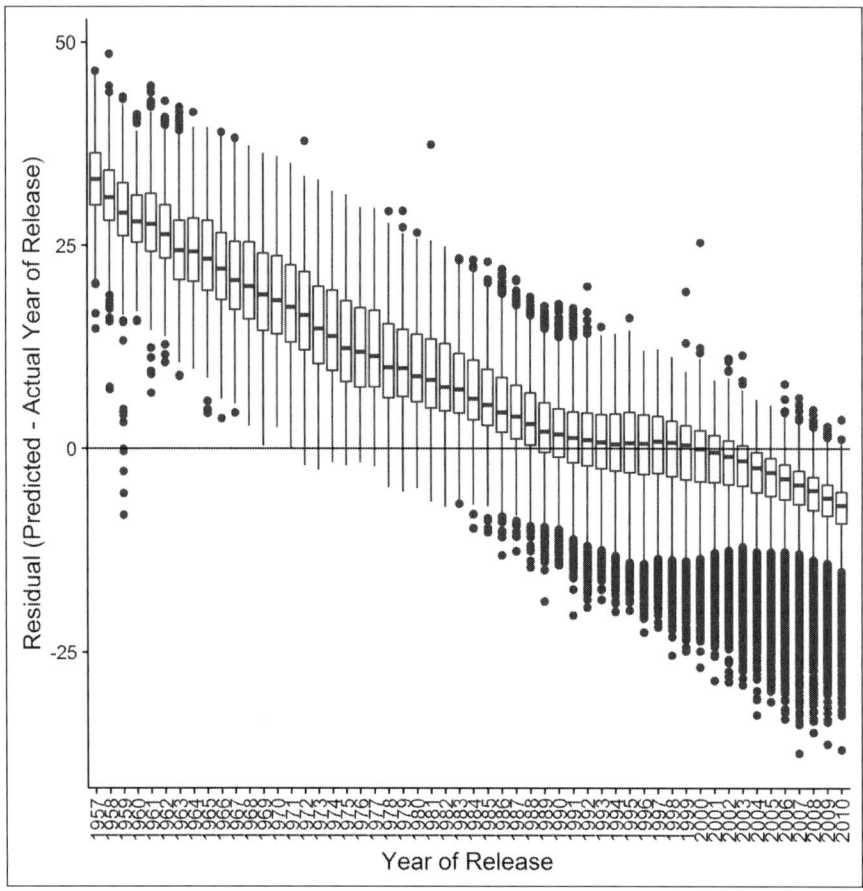

Figure 5.5

The results show a marked pattern of decreasing residuals in later years or, conversely, show extremely aberrant model predictions for the earlier years. In part, this may be due to the distribution of the data. With most cases coming from the mid 1990s to 2000s, as we saw earlier in *Figure 5.4* the model will be most sensitive to accurately predicting these values, and the comparatively fewer cases before 1990 or 1980 will have less influence.

Because we used the `variable_importances` argument, we can extract the relative importance of each variable for the model using the `h2o.varimp()` function. Although it is difficult to accurately apportion the importance of each variable, it can be helpful to provide a rough sense of which variables tend to make a larger contribution to the prediction than others. This can be a helpful way to exclude some variables that contribute very little, for example. The following code extracts the important variables, prints the top 10 (the dataset is sorted from most to least important), and makes a graph of the results to display the distribution, shown in *Figure 5.6*:

```
imp <- as.data.frame(h2o.varimp(m2))
imp[1:10, ]
```

	variable	relative_importance	scaled_importance	percentage
1	V2	1.00	1.00	0.039
2	V3	0.66	0.66	0.026
3	V4	0.53	0.53	0.020
4	V14	0.47	0.47	0.018
5	V24	0.47	0.47	0.018
6	V7	0.44	0.44	0.017
7	V37	0.40	0.40	0.016
8	V6	0.39	0.39	0.015
9	V59	0.35	0.35	0.014
10	V26	0.34	0.34	0.013

```
p.imp <- ggplot(imp, aes(factor(variable, levels = variable),
percentage)) +
  geom_point() +
  theme_classic() +
  theme(axis.text.x = element_blank()) +
  xlab("Variable Number") +
```

```
    ylab("Percentage of Total Importance")
print(p.imp)
```

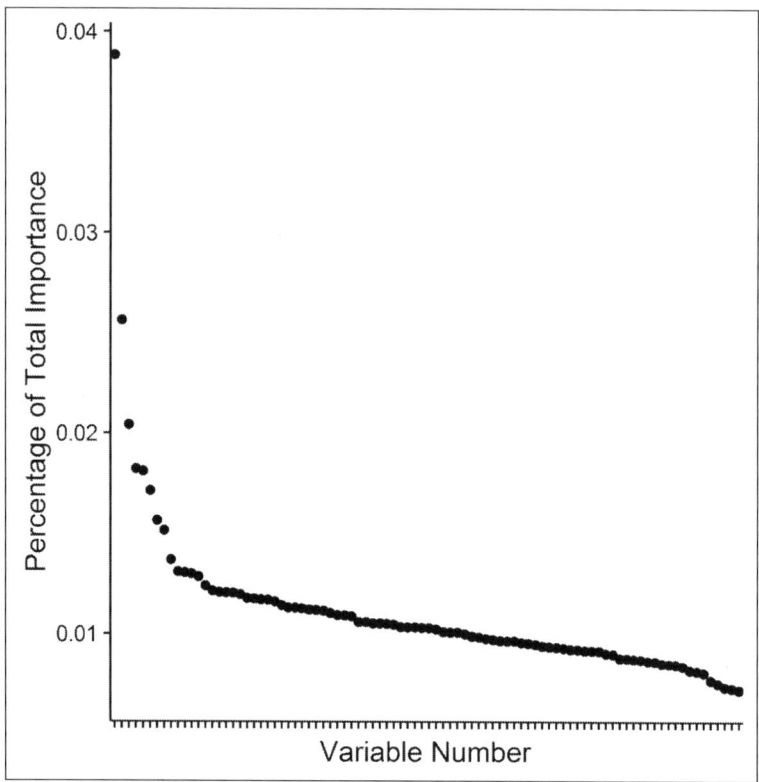

Figure 5.6

From the description of the dataset, the first 12 variables represented various timbres of the music, with the next 78 being the unique elements of a covariance matrix from the first 12. Thus it is interesting that, in the top variables, the first three are all the timbres, not from the covariances. If, for example, the later 78 variables were costly or difficult to collect, we might consider what performance is possible using only the first 12 predictors. The following model tests that approach using a simple shallow model:

```
mtest <- h2o.deeplearning(
    x = colnames(d)[2:13],
    y = "V1",
    training_frame= h2omsd.train,
```

```
  validation_frame = h2omsd.test,
  activation = "RectifierWithDropout",
  hidden = c(50),
  epochs = 100,
  input_dropout_ratio = 0,
  hidden_dropout_ratios = c(0),
  score_training_samples = 0,
  score_validation_samples = 0,
  diagnostics = TRUE,
  export_weights_and_biases = TRUE,
  variable_importances = TRUE
)
```

mtest

```
H2ORegressionModel: deeplearning
Model ID:  DeepLearning_model_R_1452082402089_15
Status of Neuron Layers: predicting V1, regression, gaussian
distribution, Quadratic loss, 701 weights/biases, 13.6 KB, 27,398,762
training samples, mini-batch size 1
  layer units          type dropout        l1        l2 mean_rate
1     1    12          Input  0.00 %
2     2    50 RectifierDropout  0.00 % 0.000000 0.000000  0.003773
3     3     1          Linear         0.000000 0.000000  0.000985
  rate_RMS momentum mean_weight weight_RMS mean_bias bias_RMS
1
2 0.007925 0.000000    0.004197   0.504967 -0.679546 0.965184
3 0.000926 0.000000   -0.106522   0.286619 -1.400430 0.000000



H2ORegressionMetrics: deeplearning
** Reported on training data. **
Description: Metrics reported on full training frame
```

```
MSE:   82
R2 :   0.24
Mean Residual Deviance :   82
```

```
H2ORegressionMetrics: deeplearning
** Reported on validation data. **
Description: Metrics reported on temporary (load-balanced) validation
frame
```

```
MSE:   83
R2 :   0.22
Mean Residual Deviance :   83
```

The results show an R^2 of only 0.24 for the training and 0.22 for the testing data. This is still comparable to the linear regression with all variables, but quite a bit lower than the 0.32 or 0.35 obtained using neural networks on the full set of predictors. Even though many of the variables have a fairly small importance, combined they add up to a noticeable difference.

Summary

In this chapter, we covered what deep neural networks are in more detail, particularly how to use them to train prediction models. Even though deep feedforward neural networks can seem quite complex, they can be broken down into a sequence of layers, each of which is fairly simple, with one set of inputs and one set of outputs, along with weights and biases to map between the two.

We have also seen the improvement in predictive performance possible using deep learning. In the use case example, using linear regression alone accounted for 23% of the variance in the testing data; however, by using a deep feedforward neural network, we were able to account for 35% of the variance in the year of song release. Although still far from perfect, it is a dramatic improvement over regression, and the low performance probably has more to do with lacking the data to explain year-to-year differences than the model itself (in other words, even with the best model achieving 99% variance accounted for is unlikely without more/better predictors). The next and final chapter will cover how to tune and optimize models, including how to address some common challenges such as missing data or poor model accuracy/performance.

6
Tuning and Optimizing Models

In this final chapter, we will discuss a few approaches to tuning models. We will cover ways of addressing missing data. Although we have used example datasets without any missing data, in the real world missing data is a common occurrence. We will also discuss what can be done when a model is performing poorly, including a detailed examination of how to search for and optimize model hyperparameters.

This chapter will cover the following topics:

- Dealing with missing data
- Solutions for models with low accuracy

In this chapter, we make use of two new packages: the **gridExtra** package for graphics and the **mgcv** package for fitting generalized additive models at the end. These new packages should be added to the checkpoint.R file, and the file should be sourced to set up the R environment for the rest of the code shown. R can be set up and an H2O cluster initialized using the following code:

```
source("checkpoint.R")
options(width = 70, digits = 2)

cl <- h2o.init(
  max_mem_size = "12G",
  nthreads = 4)
```

Dealing with missing data

When working with real-world applications, we often must contend with missing data. H2O includes a function to impute variables using the mean, median, or mode, and optionally to do so by some other grouping variables.

To examine how to impute missing data this way, we will use the small **Iris** dataset on flowers. In particular, we will set the petal width and length values to missing for the species `"setosa"` and then impute their values:

```
## setup iris data with some missing
d <- as.data.table(iris)
d[Species == "setosa", c("Petal.Width", "Petal.Length") := .(NA, NA)]

h2o.dmiss <- as.h2o(d, destination_frame="iris_missing")
h2o.dmeanimp <- as.h2o(d, destination_frame="iris_missing_imp")
```

First, we will do a simple mean imputation. This has to be done one column at a time:

```
## mean imputation
missing.cols <- colnames(h2o.dmiss)[apply(d, 2, anyNA)]

for (v in missing.cols) {
  h2o.dmeanimp <- h2o.impute(h2o.dmeanimp, column = v)
}
```

One problem with imputing the overall non-missing mean is that, if there are any systematic differences, these will be missed; also, if we could get better predictions about the missing data from any of the non-missing data, this is also missed.

Instead of a simple mean imputation, we could use a simple prediction model. The following code builds a random forest model to predict each missing column. All default values are used. If random forests take too long, a `glm` model could also be used:

```
## random forest imputation
d.imputed <- d

## prediction model
for (v in missing.cols) {
  tmp.m <- h2o.randomForest(
```

```
    x = setdiff(colnames(h2o.dmiss), v),

    y = v,

    training_frame = h2o.dmiss)

  yhat <- as.data.frame(h2o.predict(tmp.m, newdata = h2o.dmiss))

  d.imputed[[v]] <- ifelse(is.na(d.imputed[[v]]), yhat$predict,
d.imputed[[v]])

}
```

To compare the different methods, we can create a scatter plot of petal length against petal width, with the color and shape of the points determined by the flower species. This graph has three panels. The top panel is the original data. The middle panel is the data using mean imputation. The bottom panel is the data using random forest imputation. The following code creates the graph shown in *Figure 6.1*:

```
grid.arrange(
  ggplot(iris, aes(Petal.Length, Petal.Width,
    color = Species, shape = Species)) +
    geom_point() +
    theme_classic() +
    ggtitle("Original Data"),
 ggplot(as.data.frame(h2o.dmeanimp), aes(Petal.Length, Petal.Width,
    color = Species, shape = Species)) +
    geom_point() +
    theme_classic() +
   ggtitle("Mean Imputed Data"),
 ggplot(d.imputed, aes(Petal.Length, Petal.Width,
    color = Species, shape = Species)) +
    geom_point() +
    theme_classic() +
   ggtitle("Random Forest Imputed Data"),
  ncol = 1)
```

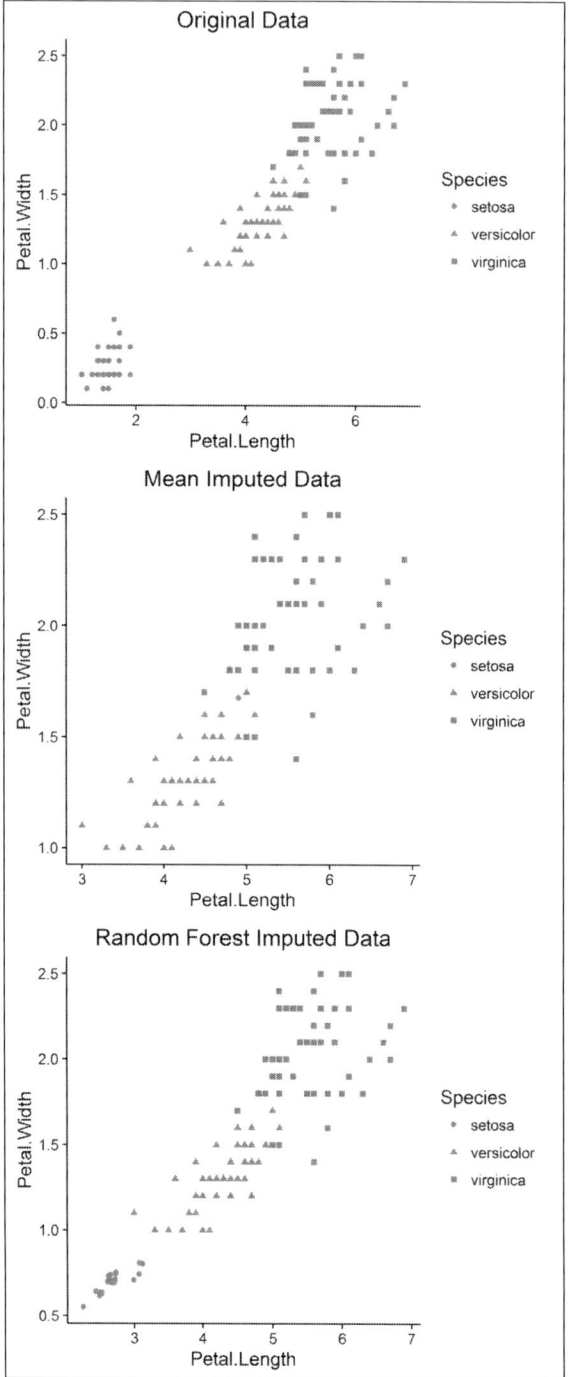

Figure 6.1

In this case, the mean imputation creates aberrant values quite removed from reality. If needed, more advanced prediction models could be generated. In statistical inferences, multiple imputation is preferred over single imputation (regardless of the method) as the latter fails to account for uncertainty—that is, when imputing the missing values there is some degree of uncertainty as to exactly what those values are. However, in most use cases for deep learning, the datasets are far too large and the computational time too demanding to create multiple datasets with different imputed values, train models on each, and pool the results; thus, these simpler methods (such as mean imputation or using some other prediction model) are common.

Solutions for models with low accuracy

One of the most challenging, but also potentially important, aspects of optimizing a model is choosing the values for the hyperparameters. In theory, we want to choose the best combination and, although we are unlikely to ever truly find the global maximum, the techniques in this section can help to find *better* values for the hyperparameters. Better hyperparameters can often improve the accuracy of a model.

Sometimes, however, a model has poor accuracy due to lacking the variables required for good prediction or because there is not enough data to support training a complex enough model to accurately predict or classify the data. In these cases, either acquiring additional variables/features that can be used as predictors and/or additional cases may be required. This book cannot help you collect more data, but it can present ways to tune and optimize hyperparameters. We'll deal with this next.

Grid search

For more information on tuning hyperparameters, see *Bengio, Y.* (2012), particularly *Section 3, Hyper-Parameters*, which discusses the selection and characteristics of various hyperparameters. Aside from manual trial and error, two other approaches to improving hyperparameters are grid searches and random searches. In a grid search, several values for hyperparameters are specified and all possible combinations are tried. This is perhaps easiest to see. In R we can use the `expand. grid()` function to create all possible combinations of variables:

```
expand.grid(
  layers = c(1, 2, 4),
  epochs = c(50, 100),
  l1 = c(.001, .01, .05))

   layers epochs     l1
```

1	1	50	0.001
2	2	50	0.001
3	4	50	0.001
4	1	100	0.001
5	2	100	0.001
6	4	100	0.001
7	1	50	0.010
8	2	50	0.010
9	4	50	0.010
10	1	100	0.010
11	2	100	0.010
12	4	100	0.010
13	1	50	0.050
14	2	50	0.050
15	4	50	0.050
16	1	100	0.050
17	2	100	0.050
18	4	100	0.050

Grid searching is excellent when there are only a few values for a few parameters. However, although this is a comprehensive way of assessing different parameter values, when there are many values for some or many parameters, it quickly becomes unfeasible. For example, even with only two values for each of eight parameters, there are $2^8 = 256$ combinations, which quickly becomes computationally impracticable. In addition, if there are no interactions between parameters and model performance, or at least the interactions are small relative to the main effects, then grid searches are an inefficient approach because many parameter values are repeated so that only a small set of values is sampled, even though many combinations are tried.

Random search

An alternative approach is searching through random sampling. Rather than pre-specifying all the values to try and creating all possible combinations, one can randomly sample values for the parameters, fit a model, store the results, and repeat. To get a very large sample size, this too would be computationally demanding, but does make it straightforward to specify just how many different models you are willing to run.

For random sampling, all that needs to be specified are the values to randomly sample or distributions to randomly draw from. Typically, some limits would also be set. For example, although a model could theoretically have any integer number of layers, some *reasonable* number (such as 1 to 10) is used rather than sampling integers from 1 to a billion.

To do random sampling, we will write a function that takes a seed and then randomly samples a number of hyperparameters, stores the sampled parameters, runs the model, and returns the results. Even though we are doing a random search to try to find better values, we are not sampling from every possible hyperparameter. Many remain fixed at values we specify or their defaults.

For some parameters, specifying how to randomly sample values can take a bit of work. For example, when using dropout for regularization, it is common to have a relatively smaller amount of dropout for the input variables (around 20% commonly) and a higher amount for hidden neurons (around 50% commonly). Choosing the right distributions can allow us to *encode* this prior information into our random search. The following code plots the density of two beta distributions, and the results are shown in *Figure 6.2*. By sampling from these distributions, we can ensure that our search, while random, focuses on small proportions of dropout for the input variables and in the 0 to 0.50 range for the hidden neurons with a tendency to over-sample from values closer to 0.50:

```
par(mfrow = c(2, 1))
plot(
  seq(0, .5, by = .001),
  dbeta(seq(0, .5, by = .001), 1, 12),
  type = "l", xlab = "x", ylab = "Density",
  main = "Density of a beta(1, 12)")

plot(
  seq(0, 1, by = .001)/2,
```

```
dbeta(seq(0, 1, by = .001), 1.5, 1),
type = "l", xlab = "x", ylab = "Density",
main = "Density of a beta(1.5, 1) / 2")
```

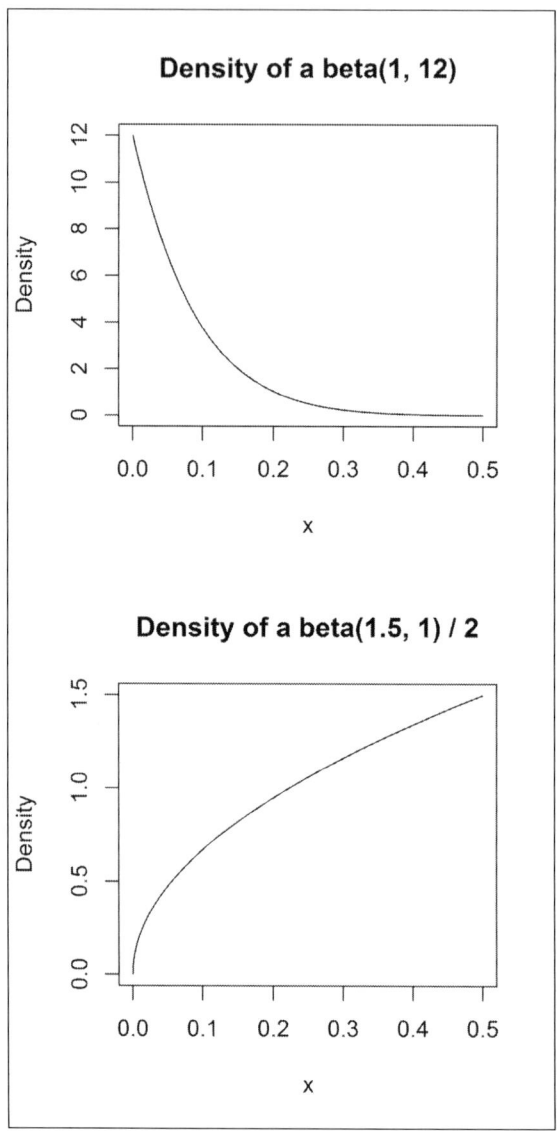

Figure 6.2

Now we can write our function, called `run()`. All it requires is a seed, which is used to make the parameter selection reproducible. A name can be specified, although there is a default based on the seed, and there is an optional (logical) argument, `run`, to control whether or not the model is run. This can be helpful if you want to check the hyperparameter values sampled.

We sample the depth or number of layers from 1 to 5 and the number of neurons in each layer from 20 to 600; by default each will have an equal probability. The `runif()` function samples from a uniform distribution in the specified range, and we have already seen the beta distribution, which we sample from using the `rbeta()` function.

Two new arguments we also randomly sample are `rho` and `epsilon`. These are used because, rather than specifying the learning rate and momentum manually, we are using (as H2O does by default) the **ADADELTA** algorithm (*Zeiler, M. D. (2012)*) to automatically tune the learning rate. ADADELTA only has two hyperparameters that need to be specified: `rho` and `epsilon`. ADADELTA works in part by examining the previous gradients but, rather than store all previous gradients, a weighted cumulative average is used. The `rho` parameter is used to weight the gradients prior to the current iteration and *1 – rho* is used to weight the gradient at the current iteration. If `rho` = 1, then the current gradient is not used and it is completely based on the previous gradients. If `rho` = 0, the previous gradients are not used and it is completely based on the current gradient. Typically, values between .9 and .999 are used.

The `epsilon` parameter is a small constant that is added when taking the root mean square of previous squared gradients to improve conditioning (it is ideal to avoid this becoming actually zero) and is typically a very small number. Further details are available from the paper presenting ADADELTA (*Zeiler, M. D. (2012)*):

```
run <- function(seed, name = paste0("m_", seed), run = TRUE) {
  set.seed(seed)

  p <- list(
    Name = name,
    seed = seed,
    depth = sample(1:5, 1),
    l1 = runif(1, 0, .01),
    l2 = runif(1, 0, .01),
    input_dropout = rbeta(1, 1, 12),
    rho = runif(1, .9, .999),
```

```
    epsilon = runif(1, 1e-10, 1e-4))


  p$neurons <- sample(20:600, p$depth, TRUE)
  p$hidden_dropout <- rbeta(p$depth, 1.5, 1)/2


  if (run) {
  model <- h2o.deeplearning(
    x = colnames(use.train.x),
    y = "Outcome",
    training_frame = h2oactivity.train,
    activation = "RectifierWithDropout",
    hidden = p$neurons,
    epochs = 100,
    loss = "CrossEntropy",
    input_dropout_ratio = p$input_dropout,
    hidden_dropout_ratios = p$hidden_dropout,
    l1 = p$l1,
    l2 = p$l2,
    rho = p$rho,
    epsilon = p$epsilon,
    export_weights_and_biases = TRUE,
    model_id = p$Name
  )


  ## performance on training data
  p$MSE <- h2o.mse(model)
  p$R2 <- h2o.r2(model)
  p$Logloss <- h2o.logloss(model)
  p$CM <- h2o.confusionMatrix(model)


  ## performance on testing data
  perf <- h2o.performance(model, h2oactivity.test)
  p$T.MSE <- h2o.mse(perf)
  p$T.R2 <- h2o.r2(perf)
  p$T.Logloss <- h2o.logloss(perf)
```

```
  p$T.CM <- h2o.confusionMatrix(perf)


} else {

  model <- NULL

}


return(list(

  Params = p,

  Model = model))

}
```

Before we can run the models, we need to load our data, which for this example is the activity data:

```
use.train.x <- read.table("UCI HAR Dataset/train/X_train.txt")

use.test.x <- read.table("UCI HAR Dataset/test/X_test.txt")


use.train.y <- read.table("UCI HAR Dataset/train/y_train.txt")[[1]]

use.test.y <- read.table("UCI HAR Dataset/test/y_test.txt")[[1]]


use.train <- cbind(use.train.x, Outcome = factor(use.train.y))

use.test <- cbind(use.test.x, Outcome = factor(use.test.y))


use.labels <- read.table("UCI HAR Dataset/activity_labels.txt")


h2oactivity.train <- as.h2o(

  use.train,

  destination_frame = "h2oactivitytrain")


h2oactivity.test <- as.h2o(

  use.test,

  destination_frame = "h2oactivitytest")
```

In order to make the parameters reproducible, we specify a list of random seeds, which we loop through to run the models:

```
use.seeds <- c(403L, 10L, 329737957L, -753102721L, 1148078598L,
-1945176688L,

-1395587021L, -1662228527L, 367521152L, 217718878L, 1370247081L,
```

```
571790939L, -2065569174L, 1584125708L, 1987682639L, 818264581L,
1748945084L, 264331666L, 1408989837L, 2010310855L, 1080941998L,
1107560456L, -1697965045L, 1540094185L, 1807685560L, 2015326310L,
-1685044991L, 1348376467L, -1013192638L, -757809164L, 1815878135L,
-1183855123L, -91578748L, -1942404950L, -846262763L, -497569105L,
-1489909578L, 1992656608L, -778110429L, -313088703L, -758818768L,
-696909234L, 673359545L, 1084007115L, -1140731014L, -877493636L,
-1319881025L, 3030933L, -154241108L, -1831664254L)
```

The models can be run (although it takes some time) simply by looping through the seeds:

```
model.res <- lapply(use.seeds, run)
```

Once the models are done, we can create a dataset, and plot the **mean squared error (MSE)** against the different parameters, using the following code. The results are shown in *Figure 6.3*:

```
model.res.dat <- do.call(rbind, lapply(model.res, function(x)
with(x$Params,
  data.frame(l1 = l1, l2 = l2,
             depth = depth, input_dropout = input_dropout,
             SumNeurons = sum(neurons),
             MeanHiddenDropout = mean(hidden_dropout),
             rho = rho, epsilon = epsilon, MSE = T.MSE)))) 


p.perf <- ggplot(melt(model.res.dat, id.vars = c("MSE")), aes(value,
MSE)) +
  geom_point() +
  stat_smooth(color = "black") +
  facet_wrap(~ variable, scales = "free_x", ncol = 2) +
  theme_classic()
print(p.perf)
```

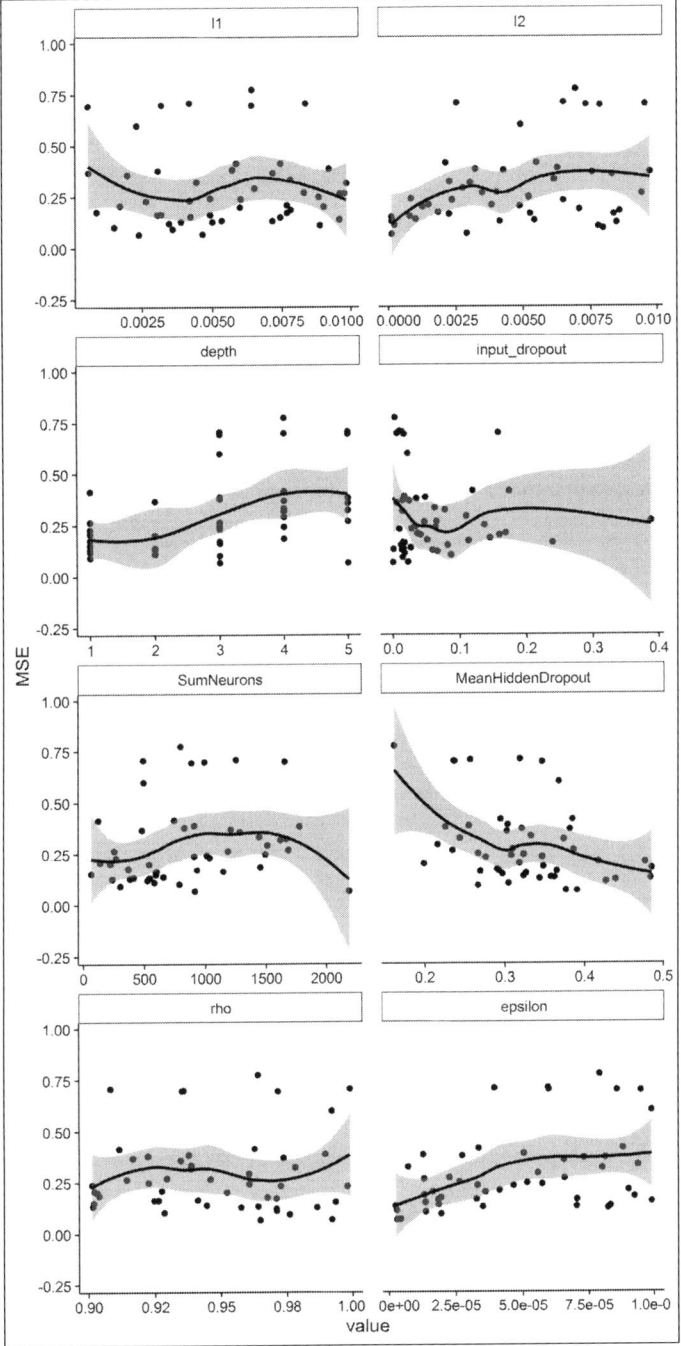

Figure 6.3

In addition to viewing the univariate relations between parameters and the model error, it can be helpful to use a multivariate model to simultaneously take different parameters into account.

To fit this (and allow some non-linearity), we use a generalized additive model, using the `gam()` function from the mgcv package. We specifically hypothesize an interaction between the model depth and total number of hidden neurons, which we capture by including both of those terms in a tensor expansion using the `te()` function, with the remaining terms given univariate smooths, using the `s()` function. The specifics here are not so important. The key is to somehow model the relation between the hyperparameters and model performance in order to decide what values should be chosen:

```
m.gam <- gam(MSE ~ s(l1, k = 4) +
             s(l2, k = 4) +
             s(input_dropout) +
             s(rho, k = 4) +
             s(epsilon, k = 4) +
             s(MeanHiddenDropout, k = 4) +
             te(depth, SumNeurons, k = 4),
           data = model.res.dat)
```

Now we can visualize the results. The first six univariate terms we plot on one graph, using the following code; this is shown in *Figure 6.4*. The constant term is not shown, so these values are not directly MSE estimates, but the key is to find the lowest point for each hyperparameter:

```
par(mfrow = c(3, 2))
for (i in 1:6) {
  plot(m.gam, select = i)
}
```

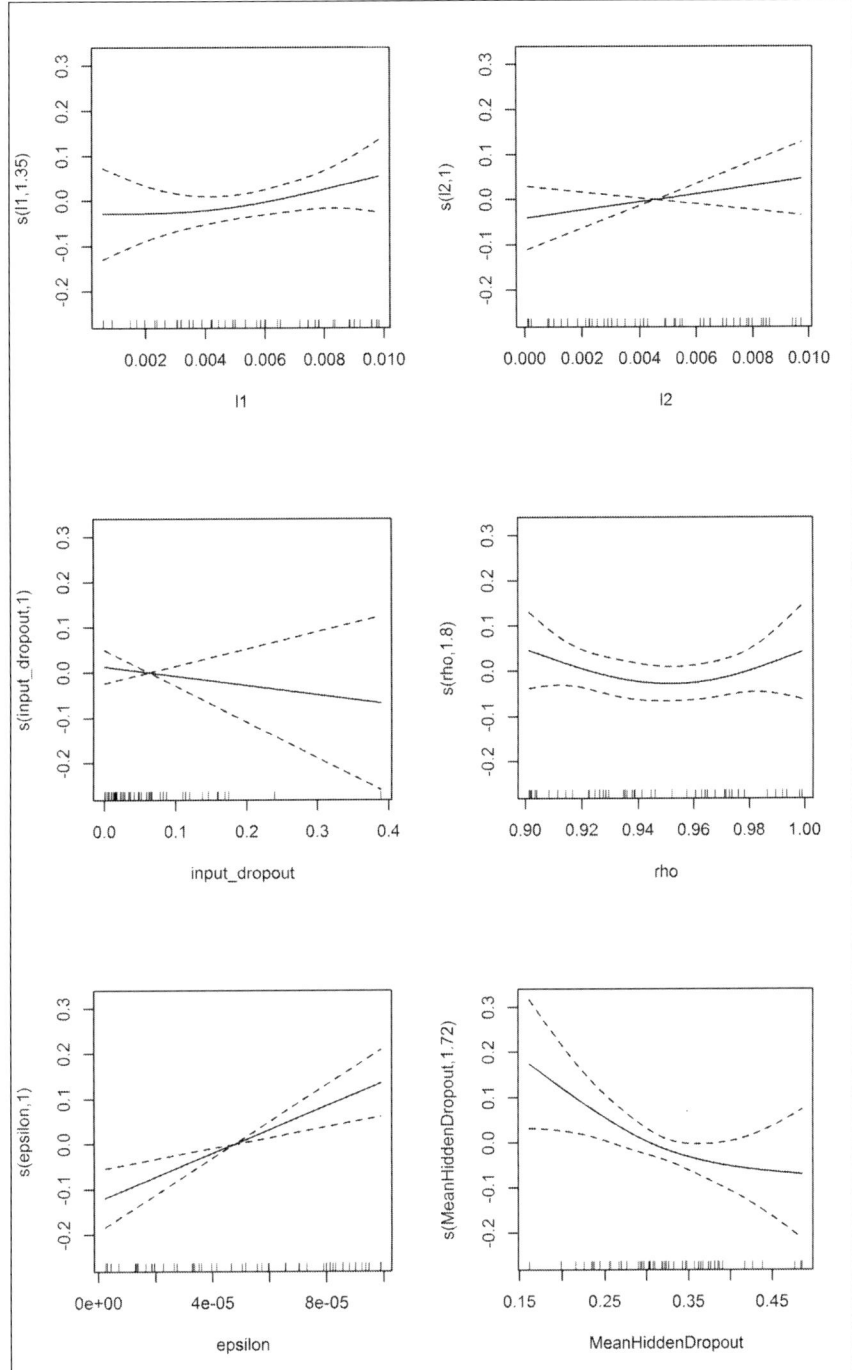

Figure 6.4

Finally, we plot the interaction term with the following code:

```
plot(m.gam, select = 7)
```

The results are shown in *Figure 6.5*. This is a contour plot and shows each variable in the interaction on the x and y axes. The actual MSE is not shown, but is labeled on the lines. Because of the interaction, it is possible to get the same estimated MSE using different combinations of the predictors. In general, it seems that, the more layers there are, the more neurons are required to achieve a comparable performance:

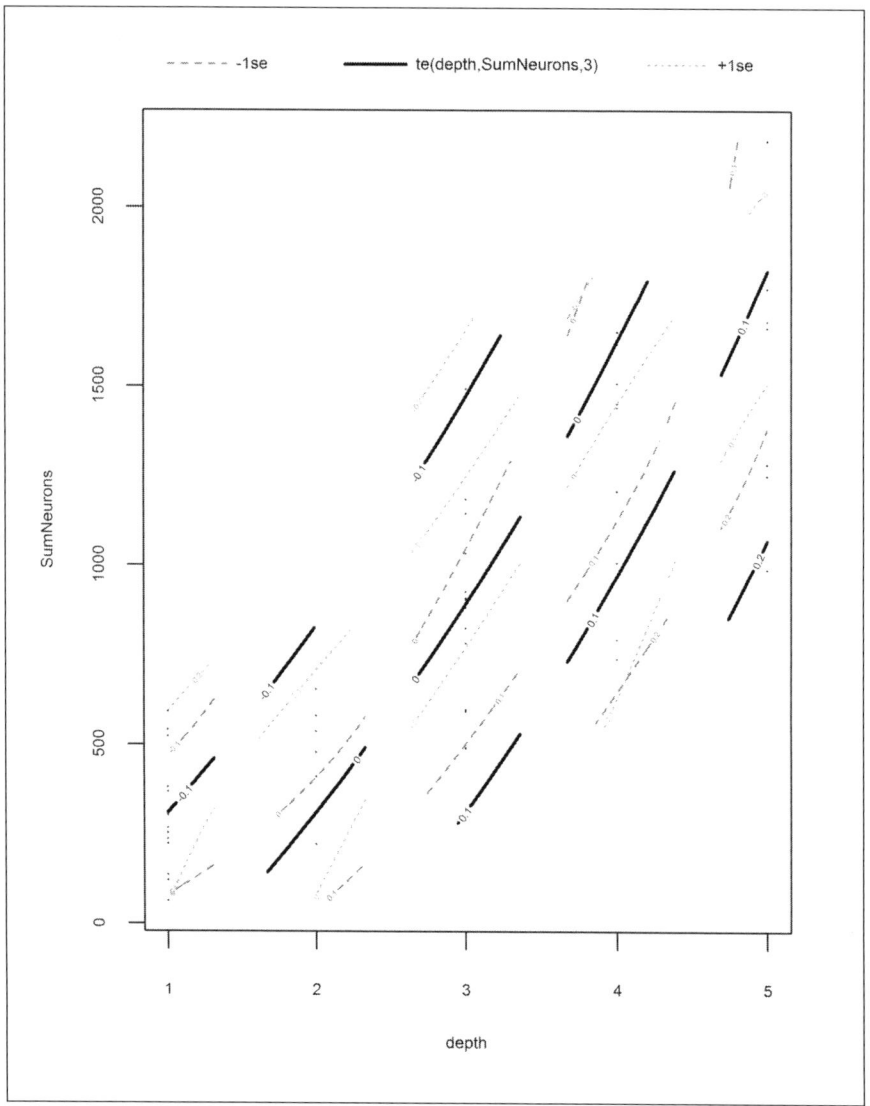

Figure 6.5

Based on these graphs, we chose hyperparameters and specify an *optimized* model in the following code:

```
model.optimized <- h2o.deeplearning(
    x = colnames(use.train.x),
    y = "Outcome",
    training_frame = h2oactivity.train,
    activation = "RectifierWithDropout",
    hidden = c(300, 300, 300),
    epochs = 100,
    loss = "CrossEntropy",
    input_dropout_ratio = .08,
    hidden_dropout_ratios = c(.50, .50, .50),
    l1 = .002,
    l2 = 0,
    rho = .95,
    epsilon = 1e-10,
    export_weights_and_biases = TRUE,
    model_id = "optimized_model"
)
```

After training, we can estimate the model performance in the validation data by using the `h2o.performance()` function and passing the optimized model and the testing data as arguments:

```
H2OMultinomialMetrics: deeplearning


Test Set Metrics:
=====================


MSE: (Extract with `h2o.mse`) 0.053
R^2: (Extract with `h2o.r2`) 0.98
Logloss: (Extract with `h2o.logloss`) 0.18
Confusion Matrix: Extract with `h2o.confusionMatrix(<model>, <data>)`)
============================================================================
      X1   X2   X3   X4   X5  X6  Error        Rate
1     491   0   5   0   0   0 0.010      5 / 496
2      12 457   1   0   1   0 0.030     14 / 471
```

```
3          32  47 341   0   0   0 0.188    79 /  420
4           0   2   0 434  55   0 0.116    57 /  491
5           0   0   0  38 494   0 0.071    38 /  532
6           0   0   0   0  15 522 0.028    15 /  537
Totals 535 506 347 472 565 522 0.071 208 / 2,947


Hit Ratio Table: Extract with `h2o.hit_ratio_table(<model>, <data>)`
========================================================================
Top-6 Hit Ratios:
   k hit_ratio
1 1   0.929420
2 2   0.993892
3 3   0.998643
4 4   0.999661
5 5   1.000000
6 6   1.000000
```

Finally, we can compare the performance of our optimized model against the single best model from the random search. Using the optimized parameters, we were able to achieve an MSE of 0.053 in the testing data, a reduction of approximately 21% from the single best model found during the random search:

```
model.res.dat[which.min(model.res.dat$MSE), ]


        l1        l2 depth input_dropout SumNeurons MeanHiddenDropout
18 0.0024 0.00011     5          1e-04       2186              0.39
      rho epsilon    MSE
18 0.96   3e-06 0.067
```

In this section we showed how to search a variety of hyperparameters and, using graphs and some modeling, how to attempt to choose better hyperparameters. It is also possible to optimize hyperparameters more formally, such as by using the Spearmint library for Bayesian optimization of hyperparameters, available online here: https://github.com/HIPS/Spearmint. Although these fine tuning and optimization examples have only been shown for deep prediction models, they can be applied to both prediction and anomaly detection.

Summary

With the techniques in *Chapter 4, Identifying Anomalous Data* and *Chapter 5, Training Deep Prediction Models*, you should be able to set up and use deep auto-encoders to learn features in data, identify outliers or anomalous values, and deep-feed forward neural networks to predict new outcomes or classify data, such as images, speech, or other data. Although just an introduction, the ideas and code from this book can get you started using deep learning to solve real-world, practical problems.

Deep learning and artificial intelligence are very active areas of research. New tools and techniques are coming out all the time and this book has only provided an introduction to some of the standard and commonly used models in deep learning. It is an exciting time to learn about this field, and I hope that this book has helped you begin your journey.

Bibliography

The following are the references for all the citations throughout the book:

- *Anguita, D., Ghio, A., Oneto, L., Parra, X., and Reyes-Ortiz, J. L. (2013). A Public Domain Dataset for Human Activity Recognition Using Smartphones. 21th European Symposium on Artificial Neural Networks, Computational Intelligence and Machine Learning, ESANN 2013.* Bruges (Belgium), 24-26 April 2013.

- *Bengio, Y. (2012). Practical Recommendations for Gradient-Based Training of Deep Architectures. In Neural Networks: Tricks of the Trade (pp. 437-478). Springer Berlin Heidelberg.* (Also on the arXiv: `http://arxiv.org/pdf/1206.5533.pdf`)

- *Bengio, Y., Courville, A., and Vincent, P. (2013). Representation Learning: A Review and New Perspectives. Pattern Analysis and Machine Intelligence, IEEE Transactions, 35(8), 1798-1828.*

- *Bergmeir, C., and Benítez, J. M. (2012). Neural Networks in R Using the Stuttgart Neural Network Simulator: RSNNS. Journal of Statistical Software, 46(7), 1-26.*

- *Bishop, C. M. (2006). Pattern Recognition and Machine Learning, Springer.*

- *Goodfellow, I. J., Warde-Farley, D., Mirza, M., Courville, A., and Bengio, Y. (2013). Maxout Networks. arXiv preprint arXiv:1302.4389.*

- *Hastie, T., Tibshirani, R., and Friedman, J. (2009). The Elements of Statistical Learning: Data Mining, Inference, and Prediction. Second Edition. Springer.*

- *Hinton, G. E., Osindero, S., and Teh, Y. W. (2006). A fast learning algorithm for deep belief nets. Neural Computation, 18 (7), 1527-1554.*

- *Kuhn, M. (2008). Building Predictive Models in R Using the caret Package. Journal of Statistical Software, 28 (5), 1-26.*

- *Kuhn, M.* and *Johnson, K.* (2013). *Applied Predictive Modeling.* New York: Springer.

- *Lichman, M.* (2013). *UCI Machine Learning Repository* (`http://archive.ics.uci.edu/ml`). Irvine, CA: University of California, School of Information and Computer Science.

- *Murphy, K. P.* (2012). *Machine Learning: A Probabilistic Perspective.* MIT press.

- *Nair, V.,* and *Hinton, G. E.* (2010). *Rectified Linear Units Improve Restricted Boltzmann Machines.* In *Proceedings of the 27th International Conference on Machine Learning* (ICML-10) (pp. 807-814).

- *Riedmiller, M.,* and *Braun, H.* (1993). *A Direct Adaptive Method for Faster Backpropagation Learning: The RPROP Algorithm.* In *Neural Networks, 1993,* IEEE International Conference.

- *Schmidhuber, J.* (2015). *Deep Learning in Neural Networks: An Overview. Neural Networks,* 61, 85-117.

- *Srivastava, N., Hinton, G., Krizhevsky, A., Sutskever, I.,* and *Salakhutdinov, R.* (2014). *Dropout: A Simple Way to Prevent Neural Networks from Overfitting. The Journal of Machine Learning Research,* 15(1), 1929-1958.

- *Venables, W. N.* and *Ripley, B. D.* (2002). *Modern Applied Statistics with S-Plus. Fourth Edition. Springer.*

- *Vincent, P., Larochelle, H., Bengio, Y.,* and *Manzagol, P. A.* (2008, July). *Extracting and Composing Robust Features with Denoising Autoencoders.* In *Proceedings of the 25th International Conference on Machine Learning* (pp. 1096-1103). ACM.

- *Zeiler, M. D.* (2012). *ADADELTA: An Adaptive Learning Rate Method.* arXiv preprint arXiv:1212.5701.

Index

A

ADADELTA algorithm 139
auto-encoders
  applying 88
  building 84-88
  data.table package, adding 71
  denoising 71
  models, fine-tuning 88-93
  overcomplete 70
  penalized 70
  regularized 70
  training, in R 71-83
  undercomplete 69
  use case 84
  working 69
automatic classification
  deep neural network, training for 112-121

B

bagging 60
bibliography 151, 152

C

caret package 19
Classification and Regression Training 19
Comprehensive R Archive Network (CRAN)
  about 9
  URL 9
Convolutional Neural Network (CNN) 8

D

darch package 13
datasets
  linking, to H2O cluster 15-17
Deep Belief Networks (DBNs) 6
deep feedforward neural networks 96-98
deep learning
  about 2
  deep neural network (DNN) 6-8
  neural networks 2-5
deep learning, R packages
  about 8
  darch package 13
  deepnet package 12
  H2O package 13
  neural networks 12
  reproducible results, setting up 9-12
deep neural network (DNN)
  about 6
  model results, working with 123-130
  new data, predicting 104-112
  new data, training 104-112
  training, for automatic
      classification 112-121
  URL 112
dropout
  defining 60-64

E

Emacs Speaks Statistics (ESS) 8
ensembles
  and model averaging 57-60
epochs 73

F

feedforward neural networks 96

G

ggplot2 package 78
glmnet 50
grandmother cell 2
gridExtra package 131

H

H2O
  about 1, 13
  datasets, linking 15, 16
  initializing 14, 15
  URL 9
H2O package 13
hidden neurons 4
Hogwild!
  URL 73
hyperbolic tangent 98
hyperparameters
  picking 100-103

I

inputs 4
integrated development environment
  (IDE) 8
Iris dataset 132

K

Kaggle 20
K-means clustering 68

L

L1 penalty
  defining 48, 49
  working 50-52
L2 penalty
  defining 52
  weight decay 54-56
  working 53, 54
learning rate 22

Least Absolute Shrinkage and Selection
  Operator (lasso) 48

M

maxout 98
mean squared error (MSE) 75, 142
mgcv package 131
Million Song Dataset 112
missing data
  dealing with 132-135
model averaging
  and ensembles 57-60
models
  grid search 135, 136
  random search 137-148
  with low accuracy, solutions 135
Modified National Institute of Standards
  and Technology (MNIST) 62, 72, 100

N

neural network (NN)
  about 2-6
  applying 40-45
  building 20-33, 40-45
  in R 19, 20
  predictions, generating from 35-37
nnet 19

O

Ordinary Least Squares (OLS) 48
overfitting data problem
  about 37
  consequences 38-40

P

predictions
  about 2
  generating, from neural network 35-37

R

R
  and H2O, connecting 13
rectifier 98

Recurrent Neural Network (RNN) 8, 96
Restricted Boltzmann Machine (RBM) 6
R package checkpoint 9
RSNNS 12, 19
Rstudio 8

S

Spearmint library
  URL 148
Stuttgart Neural Network Simulator
      (SNNS) 12, 32
supervised learning 68

U

unsupervised learning 68, 69

V

Vincent Goulet
  URL 8

Printed in Great Britain
by Amazon